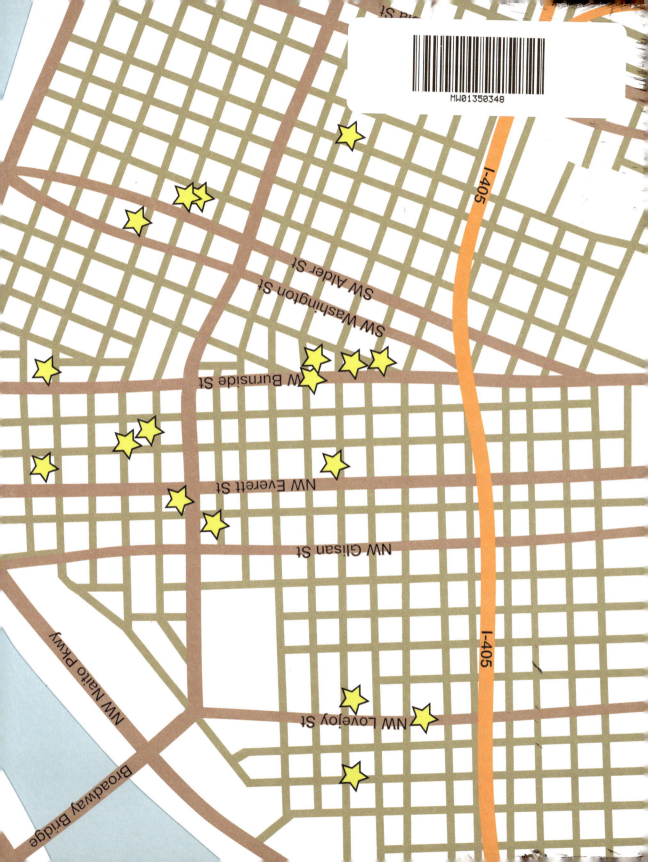

The Best Places to PEE

A GUIDE TO THE FUNKY & FABULOUS BATHROOMS OF PORTLAND

KELLY MELILLO

First Edition
ISBN 978-0-9851893-0-3
Copyright 2013

Silent 7 Publishing

The Best Places To Pee: A Guide To The Funky & Fabulous Bathrooms Of Portland
www.thebestplacestopee.com
All Rights Reserved

Printed in The United States of America

Cover Photo: Vivian Johnson
Cover Design: Stefanie Fontecha www.beetiful.com

No part of this book may be reproduced in any form without written permission from the author.

Great effort was taken to ensure all the information in this book is 100% accurate and up-to-date as of the press date; however, things can and do change rapidly in the restaurant industry. So before you set up a "loo tour," it never hurts to double check the facts before you "gotta go."

Special Sales

The Best Places To Pee: A Guide To The Funky & Fabulous Bathrooms Of Portland is available at special discounts on bulk purchases for corporate, club or organization sales promotions, premiums, and gifts.

For more information, contact Silent 7 Publishing
girlonthegopdx@gmail.com

The Loo Crew

Author and Photographer………………..………………………..Kelly Melillo
Editor ………………………………………………………………......Rachel Guerin
Book Design………………………………………..............................Craig Williams

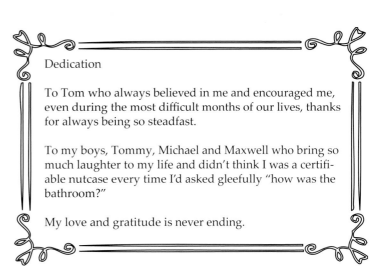

Dedication

To Tom who always believed in me and encouraged me, even during the most difficult months of our lives, thanks for always being so steadfast.

To my boys, Tommy, Michael and Maxwell who bring so much laughter to my life and didn't think I was a certifiable nutcase every time I'd asked gleefully "how was the bathroom?"

My love and gratitude is never ending.

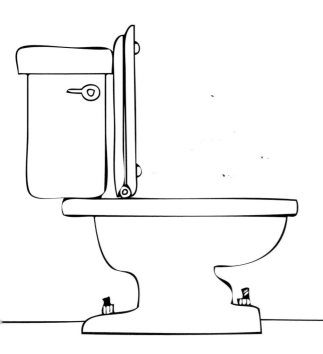

Foreword

When is a Bathroom Not Just a Bathroom?

As a small boy, my family would dine at Benihana Restaurant. It was a showcase of flair and craftsmanship, part serious Japanese restaurant and part Asian American kitsch. While seated around the huge metal cooking surface, I would watch in awe as the chef prepared our dinner. Fast and precise, cooking multiple dishes at once, it was always a delicious spectacle. But for me, the magic of Benihana was not just in its food and its theatrical presentation, but above all, in its bathrooms. The men's room was small—just one urinal and a stall—painted an intense red with bright gold trim.

As a functioning bathroom, it was not much to behold, but the walls were covered with 8"x10" pictures of Benihana's founder, Rocky Aoki, either in a tuxedo or a speed boat racing outfit alongside some of Hollywood's finest. There were dozens of them and they told a tale of success—perhaps even excess—and American celebrity pop culture. Everyone from Loni Anderson to Sammy Davis, Jr. was there, and it was those photos that would take my basic human need to be in the bathroom and transport me to a world of '70s celebrity and paparazzi. I use that story to illustrate the transformative power of a well-designed bathroom. On a basic level, both bathrooms and restaurants satisfy primal human needs. But like any art, each in and of itself can take the mundane and transmit it to ethereal heights.

This book serves to capture the restaurant bathroom as an objet d'art. Each offers its base purpose and yet, can also afford humanity an aesthetic experience that can serve multiple purposes beyond the basic: perhaps a sanctuary from a horrific first date, perhaps a place to reflect and digest the restaurant experience.

My own personal opinion would suggest that a well-designed bathroom should reflect the restaurant itself, perhaps even frame the ethos of the restaurant establishment. Either way, it should strive to diminish the profane aspect of our humanity and elevate us to see, seek, and share.

- Jason French, Owner of Ned Ludd

Introduction

Growing up, I never had aspirations to be "The Lady of the Loo" or imagined myself a water closet connoisseur. Yet here I am, well versed with facts and trivia about the porcelain of Portland. How does a Midwest girl with a Criminal Justice degree get to become a Pacific Northwestern with a penchant for potties? A cross-country move, mass amounts of coffee and water, and an endearing proclivity for the unconventional.

Every once in awhile we encounter a moment when our typical perspective is altered and we see items, landscapes, or situations in a different light. The ordinary becomes something more . . . Bathrooms are places you enter out of necessity without expecting anything other than the usual white porcelain amenities. So when you walk into a restroom for the first time and find yourself wowed, awed, and even bewildered, it makes an impression. And that's exactly how this project was born: out of a lasting impression after I walked into the ladies room at The Doug Fir.

Porcelain proved to be the perfect catalyst for what evolved into a gleaming example of a six-degrees-of-water-closet separation game. Inevitably a visit to one ordinary john, followed by a casual conversation with a bartender segued to the whereabouts of a local legendary loo.

Other people's enthusiasm further fueled my fascination and piqued my curiosity to discover just how many funky and fabulous bathrooms I could uncover.

At first, it was the unusual, artistic, or humorous nature of these bathrooms that caught my attention. But as I started to talk with the staff and owners of these establishments, it was then that the underlying character of the book really began to take shape. What I uncovered were bathrooms that tell a story (Salt & Straw), water closets that embody an owner's personality (The Gilt Club), loos that are tinged with humor (Binks), and thoughtfully curated to extend your dining experience and convey a story (Ned Ludd).

The Best Places to Pee: A Guide to the Funky & Fabulous Bathrooms of Portland is a blend of whimsical inspiration and eccentric exploration, offering up a quirky concoction of colorful and witty narratives that in turn reveal an alluring mix of history, folklore, and personal insights. This offbeat book's distinctive sketch of Portland lovingly mirrors the city's renowned reputation as one of the most irreverent and popular places to visit and live.

- Kelly Melillo

Ned Ludd

Jason French, the owner of Ned Ludd, works under the umbrella of ingenuity and spontaneity. He created a rustically chic dining room, which channels a modern day workshop replete with weathered wood furnishings, exposed beams, vintage light fixtures, and glassware. A wood-fire oven remained from a failed pizza joint that was previously housed here.

Equipped with the wood-fired oven, a two-burner hot plate, a small alto sham, and a steam table, the "kitchen" clearly operates on wood, not gas, churning out memorable meals that keep throngs of faithful and curious diners flooding the restaurant nightly.

Seasonality is key here with ingredients changing weekly. A garden planted out back supplements the ingredients sourced from local markets and farms. Rainwater is collected to help water the garden, bins of fruitwood (fuel for the oven) outline the seating area in front of the restaurant, and hints at the farm-driven rustic cuisine that awaits you inside.

As expressed in the foreword to this book, French believes bathrooms are an extension of one's dining experience beyond the food, the service and your dining companions. The bathrooms at Ned Ludd are a vestige of an era gone-by, reflective of French's fondness for

antiquity and beauty. Turquoise and yellow canvas the walls and charming one-off items collectively displayed within the bathroom tell a story.

Both washrooms embody the pioneering movement of a generation that dealt with hard times in exchange for the plethora of possibilities awaiting them. This is seen in the faces of the vintage photos (including a photograph of French's dad), seasoned tools, doses of humor (such as the rap poster hung in a gold Goodwill frame), and an abundance of organic elements that fill every corner of these one-room odysseys.

This pioneering spirit is reflective of French himself. His journey has taken him thousands of miles while accruing hundreds of experiences that have culminated in incredible joy and success as a restaurateur.

The Gilt Club

The Gilt Club is decadent and stylish, without coming off as pretentious. Oversized red booths and art deco chandeliers are reminiscent of the roaring '20s. The cocktail list follows suit with delightfully pleasing cocktails from the prohibition era, such as, "The Blood and Sand," "The Scafflaw," and "The Gilt Manhattan." This luxurious eatery doubles as a late-night supper club that serves gourmet food into the wee hours of the morning. Order their "Foie Gras Torchon PB and J" just before 2 AM—because sometimes one's palate is in the mood for something a little more grown up than a "run for the border."

The Gilt Club eagerly adapts to suit your evening's agenda. Celebrating an anniversary and want a great bottle of champagne in a cozy booth back in the corner? Done. Planning a dinner with friends who love to share plates? The Gilt is an ideal stop. Heading up the street to see a play and want a pre-show drink? Choose a seat at the bar, order a classic cocktail, and your evening has just started off smashingly.

Jamie Dunn, the owner of The Gilt Club, has been deemed the weirdest boss ever by his unwaveringly candid staff. Dunn is known for having an abundance of odd and infectiously endearing traits like: wearing gold and silver shoes; responding to important and sometimes urgent questions with "Bleep, bloop, blop. I am an interstellar robot;" and being a sarcastic perfectionist with a passion for kitschy collectibles.*

Aside from these captivatingly odd traits, Jamie Dunn is no slouch. He opened his first restaurant in Chicago at 24, and his second restaurant was featured in The Chicago Tribune's "Ten Best New Restaurants." Dunn's passions brought him out west and he soon found himself envisioning and creating another superb restaurant. The design of The Gilt Club was entirely conceived by Dunn and he also did the majority of the buildout, occasionally channeling his inner robot for help computing measurements and layout logistics. Pretty impressive for a gold-shoe-wearing, moody perfectionist with a sweet tooth.

The Gilt Club's restrooms seem to take their lead from Dunn's comical, yet sophisticated persona. They are tasteful with a splash of unconventionality. Enter the restroom, flip the light switch, and you'll see terra cotta colored walls with iridescent glazed stripes and a hammered copper sink: classy and vogue. Ah but wait! Within three seconds—just long enough for your brain to recognize and be startled by the new addition to your surroundings—you may hear a voice or two, perhaps instructions on how to breakdance, or a request to spell "preternatural." No, it's not another quirky trait of Dunn's to follow customers into the restroom—the voices you hear in the john come from a vintage record player mounted overhead and hardwired to turn on with the lights. The records range from Jean-Luc Ponty's album, "A Taste for Passion," recordings of spelling bees, foreign language lessons, and other random tracks. Both bathrooms have vintage record players, but only one has a full-sized, free-play video game. Why put a video game in the bathroom? Why not? Bleep, Bloop, Blop!

* The sale of his Pez collection garnered him a sum large enough to be used as a down payment for his home! Now that's one hell of a lot of pez, peoples!

Rontoms

Rontoms is located on the busy corner of East Burnside and 6th Avenue, with no definitive sign, no hours listed and an indistinguishable entrance; your clue to finding it is their obscure logo: a man with a propeller strapped to his back painted on the building's façade.

Once setting your sights on the propeller man, you'll enter to find a cavernous room with high ceilings and wood-hewed walls. The lounge is lit with an abundance of flickering candles, and intimate seating vignettes are scattered throughout the room. The space screams 1969 cocktail party with its low-slung chairs, couches and lustrous polyurethane surfaces that reflect and refract the candlelight. Floor lamps that bobble and sway, table lamps with shades as big as toddlers, and a color palette of mustard yellow, mossy green, burnt orange, and red add to the retro vibe. Centered in this space is a sunken living room of sorts, with couches and chairs lining the perimeter, complemented by a fireplace that anchors and enhances its living room quality. The food also mimics the retro vibe with plates such as deviled eggs, Swedish meatballs and fondue.

The owner, Ron Tom (yes, that is actually his name), worked as a designer before tackling the restaurant business. Tom's talent and solid vision created a gathering space that encourages its patrons to relax and linger. Weekly events consistently draw in crowds of friends for food, mingling, and lingering. A projection screen unfurls to host movie night, and local bands play front and center in the living room during free weekly Rontom Sundays. On Portland's sunnier days, the sizable patio out back is bustling with people. Large potted bamboo plants soften the hard lines and skyline of this urban oasis. Sail cloth canopies create artistic shade overhead, while a ping pong table adds entertainment and a little lively competition. A great selection of local spirits stocks the teak bar and the interior walls boast vibrant local art pieces.

This arty vibe courses its way into the restrooms. The tall walls of the ladies room are amplified with a silvery metallic forest of birch trees that shimmer and reflect the light from the chartreuse pendant light fixture and opposite walls of the same color. The men's room contains four large detailed sketches of faces, skillfully rendered by local artist Kris Hargis. These countenances create so much room for interpretation, it's a shame they are tucked away behind a closed door. Most men never even realize these sketches are on the wall in their restroom, so make sure to take a peek while you take a leek . . .

Rimsky Korsakoffee

Called "Rimsky's" by regulars, this coffee and dessert shop is housed in an old Victorian house in Southeast Portland. Its decadent desserts, cryptic décor, and haunted history have kept customers coming to this Portland landmark for 25 years. Its inconspicuous location usually leaves most inexperienced patrons circling the block a couple times before they find it. Don't be discouraged by its limited hours, lack of advertising, dark on-street parking: once you find Rimsky's, you'll be glad you did.

Rimsky's proprietress, Goody Cable*, considers herself an "assimilator of the mundane," weaving and collecting stories that make their way into this peculiar place. Each dining table is named after a deceased composer and topped with a moveable glass top so patrons can add their own mementos, which keeps the dining room's décor constantly evolving, much like Rimsky's menu. Curiously odd items hang from the ceiling—see if you can determine their common denominator. Live classical music is played almost nightly on the living room's baby grand piano.

Cable professes the house is haunted by its former owners: a couple, both writers, who witnessed the Russian revolution. Correspondingly, it has been purported that several tables at the café exhibit odd behavior, such as levitating and turning ever so stealthily. Patrons have reported that, after getting lost in conversation, they'll notice that their dessert has mysteriously made its way to the place setting in front of their companion (whether this is on the part of supernatural forces or hungry dates, we cannot confirm). The frosting on Rimsky's not-so-proverbial cake of odd ingredients is what awaits you on the second floor in the Erik Satie inspired bathroom. If you go with friends who have not seen these pictures, don't give away the surprise that awaits them through the door—just follow them up and listen to their startled squeal as they flip the light switch on.

With homemade desserts served by sassy servers, and a bathroom that will fright and delight, Rimsky's is a one-of-a-kind Portland spot worth the trip.

* Goody Cable also co-owns the literary-themed (and equally eccentric) Sylvia Beach Hotel in Newport, OR.

Casa del Matador

When I hear the word "matador," the adjectives grace, skill, and valiance come to mind. Those characteristics are apparent when you step through the doors of Casa del Matador East Burnside. The interior borrows from classic Mexicana and Texan proportions. The hand-crafted wooden bar and iron accents are strong and graceful. The painted bull skulls that decorate the restaurant's walls are symbolic of the matador's brazen cunningness to willingly confront an animal that outweighs him by 80 times or more.

The Matador restaurant exhibits its own admirable skills with its innovative food, noteworthy drinks, and attentive service. Warm amber light from the custom centralized fireplace reflects the detailed stained glass work above the bar. The Matador is also a tequila bar, stocked with an extensive array of quality tequilas. The bartenders can and will educate you on this intoxicating, flammable liquid that, if you're not careful, will forever be referenced as the "I don't remember doing that!" drink.

Perhaps you sampled too many tequilas and decided to grab a decorative bull by its horn; maybe you spilled your drink hoisting yourself up on the bar in an effort to prove your own fearlessness—either way, make sure you find your way to the Latin-inspired bathrooms to freshen up.

Brushed-steel stall doors intermingle with hand-stained wood panels and glowing golden walls in the women's restroom. Bold red walls scream of bravado in the men's room. Ornate mirrors decorate and reflect, while flickering votive candles and flowers add flare to both spaces. The shape and feel of the cement vanities balance the feminine and masculine characteristics in these baños. These restrooms incarnate the audacious character of the traditional Spanish Matador.

The Side Street Tavern

Taking the side street often leads you to places with authenticity and a style that veers away from the typical. When people discover these gems, they continue to go back because of the gratification they gained by following the road less traveled.

The Side Street Tavern is a vibrant neighborhood bar that prides itself on fresh-squeezed cocktails, local beer, and being nice to its customers. The facilities at The Side Street reflect management's affection for their costumers as well as their confidence that their patrons are witty and entertaining. Chalkboard walls are not new to bathrooms and one can easily deduce that creating these kinds of walls cuts down on the typical penchant some bar patrons have for graffiti. A shiny silver bucket of colored chalk sits in the corner of this colorful create-your-own-wallpaper bathroom, anxiously awaiting another fondling by the next exuberant artist. With almost every toilet flush, art magically appears on the walls in the form of masterpieces that entertain rather than offend. These walls tell a story through skillful images created from affinities with pop culture, whimsical sayings written in foreign languages, and playful drawings of objects that produce smiles (and lingering bathroom visits).

Advice for those who plan to spend some quality time in this water closet: if you are going to make people wait in line while you're leaving your mark on the walls, it better be good! And consider this a public service announcement: the bucket is indeed filled with colored chalk, not candies, as the poor guy who exited the bathroom with multi-colored-chalk-stained-teeth quickly learned.

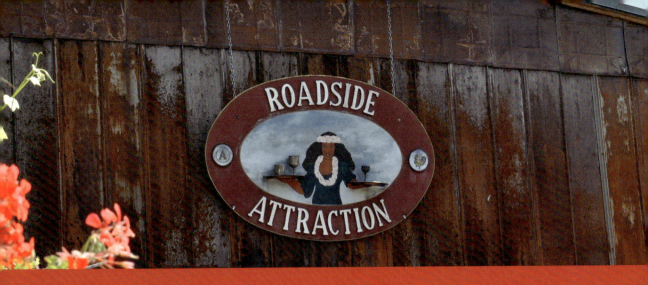

Roadside Attraction

Roadside Attraction is a local bar that has succeeded in living up to its name. As you drive by, you can't help but gawk at all the odds and ends that overflow onto the sidewalk and bait you to explore beyond its wooden fence. If your curiosity's been piqued, and you manage to find parking, your inner adventurer will be pleased. Not only will you find the large patio with a fire pit, flowering vines, and exotic flower arrangements meticulously well kept, most will find the massive collection of mismatched attractions curiously captivating.

After hosting many a party in their living room, owners Alf Evers and Peggy Barr decided to turn their house into a uniquely homey bar in Southeast Portland. Evers jubilantly explained that he had "the bar and booze installed way before they ever opened their doors as a business." Clearly the essence of Roadside Attraction was embedded in this dwelling's foundation long before its doors were open to the public.

The bathrooms here are an extension of the bar's overall experience. The ladies room offers a taste of the islands with a Hawaiian motif that errs on the classic vintage side rather than Pacific Island kitsch. Hula girls with inviting smiles, out-stretched arms, and luscious looking leis are captured in gilded frames as you enter the spacious rose-colored washroom. A fresh and exotic flower arrangement and sweet-smelling powder room products make you feel unexpectedly pampered—this is not your average neighborhood bar bathroom.

Atlas Tattoo

Atlas Tattoo resides in a seemingly unassuming building in Albina, Oregon—but its legacy is rich and eccentric, with a bathroom that aptly embodies it. The building was once home to the Albina Saloon, an alleged brothel and confirmed gathering place for stevedores, railroad men, and gamblers. It was also home to a shoe repair shop, a hardware store, and the home office for Snipe Hunt, a late '80s/early '90s music magazine. In 2005 the Atlas crew put down their ink guns and picked up their nail guns to renovate the building and make it their new home. The six tattoo artists, Jerry Ware, Lewis Hess, Cheyenne Sawyer, Jacob Redmond, Corey

Crowley, Dan Gilsdorf—as well as the indispensable shop manager, Nic Eldridge—represent over a hundred years of tattooing experience. Together, this group cultivates the perfect blend of traditional tattooing sensibilities with bold, lasting art, creating highly-coveted ink in an atmosphere of raucous banter that ranges from philosophical debates to sudden outbursts of animal noises.

Like the shop itself, its bathroom is an ever-evolving collection of intriguing oddities. A bright red tattooed door invites you in to a menagerie of taxidermy wildlife. A bobcat soars overhead towards an unsuspecting deer, while a black crow looks on from its perch. A mermaid, Jesus, and a samurai also bear witness to this calamity. Many of the items in the loo are gifts from customers and friends of the shop—displayed in a somewhat random and very imaginative narrative. Colorful tattoo art, curious knick-knacks and peculiar pictures line the walls and fill the powder-room peruser with curiosity.

Rae Bidet

NKDBY

THEY LIVE WE GROUT

Plaster People got outta my way

KLOTZ

Grout potato Grout out!

Kcandoit

Grout of this

CASKET

21st Avenue Bar and Grill

Vandalism is a worthy opponent to bar owners on a shoestring budget. Combine that vandalism with just the right texture on a bathroom wall and a phenomenon is born.

Since 1998, 21st Avenue Bar and Grill, has been "the neighborhood joint" in Northwest Portland with a chameleon-like tendency to assume the personality of its clientele. This is due mainly to its men's room: a comedic celebration of the word "grout" all over its tattered walls.

What began with the phrase "grout Scott!" in black sharpie many years ago, has been followed by other additions inspired by the initial mystery author. "Into the grout wide open," "grout at the devil," and "Mike Tyson's punch grout" are just a few among a litany of others that now decorate the bathroom. Fresh coats of paint over the grout quotes have only led to new contributions, much to the owner's chagrin.

No one seems to know who first penned "grout Scott" and initiated this enduring force, but it wasn't the staff. The loyal, tenured crew battled unsuccessfully, along with the ownership, to quell damage to their little establishment—they are now resigned to the fact that they will never grout-it-out. Those remarkable people, along with the bar's chill outdoor patio, tasty sliders and spoon-licking-good mac-n-cheese, are a worthy representation of Northwest 21st Avenue.

Five of the staff members here have been on the payroll for at least ten years, which is utterly commendable in this industry. In an era of expensive trends and attitudes, 21st Avenue Bar and Grill's friendly and unassuming consistency endures. Owner Matt Cordova has accepted his establishment's groutisms: though "frustrating and weird at times," he confesses, the 21st Avenue Bar is still "the 'groutest' place we'd ever want to own."

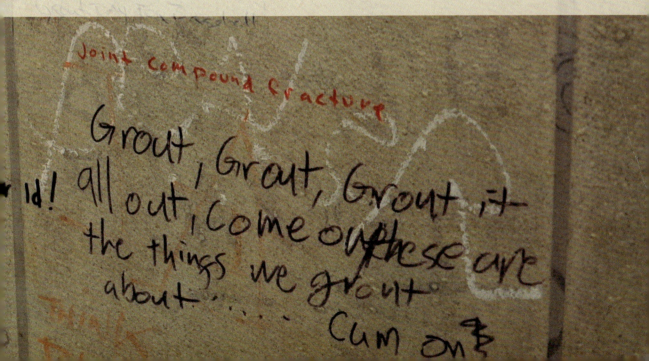

Binks

Binks' owners, Justin and Bianca Youngers, consider their bar an extension of their living room, and accordingly, they regard their patrons as their extended family. Binks has been an Alberta Street fixture for over a decade and has the reputation for the friendliest bartenders in town—even on their most bustling nights. Their cozy and intimate fireplace nook and tequila toddies invite chilled and slightly soggy Pacific Northwesterners indoors during the winter months. And when the sunshine returns and dries up the puddles, garage doors open up wide to allow the welcomed rays in. During these summer months, Binks' tables spill out onto Alberta, creating inviting sidewalk seating—ideal for art-district people watching. Fresh-squeezed juice and house-infused vodkas combine to create refreshing and inventive cocktails.

What does "Binks" mean? The true story is sweet and simple: it was owner Bianca's childhood nickname. The alternate story Bianca likes to spin is that Binks is an ancient Chinese

remedy for a hangover. The Youngers' wit goes beyond cleverly woven tales of herbs and ancient Chinese secrets.

The bathroom just beyond the colorfully-painted archway is home to the infamous "lift-the-skirt girl." What appears to be a plain wooden plaque, painted with a simple and unassuming rendering of a girl with a wooden skirt, is not as simple and unassuming as it seems . . . If, in the privacy of the bathroom, you should find yourself curiously intrigued by the thought, "just what is hiding under that hinged skirt?" go ahead and lift it! You'll soon find . . . absolutely nothing! Hmmm . . . although you see nothing, the patrons sitting at the bar adjacent to the john see a bright yellow light turn on, signaling to everyone that you have a slightly naughty curiosity when you think no one is looking. Depending on the crowd who has taken up residence at the bar during your inquisitive exploration, don't be surprised if you walk out to a round of rollicking banter, incited by your quest to explore.

Hopworks BikeBar

Portland is the home to over 40 breweries—more than any other city in the world. Lending itself to nicknames like "Beervana" and "Brewtopia," Portland is also consistently named the number one city in the country for cycling. Put those two attributes together, lease space along the bike commuter route in an eco-friendly building in North Portland, and you have an environmentally conscious, family-friendly, ingenious concept for a bar. BikeBar is the outpost of the well-known, much loved Hopworks Urban Brewery on Southeast Powell Boulevard (see p. 68).

Hopworks BikeBar sits along the main bike commuter route on North Williams Avenue—known to cyclists as "the bike highway." A staggering 3,000 bike commuters utilize this route on a daily basis. Paying homage to these cyclists and adhering to the eco-consciousness of today's lifestyles, BikeBar was created to exemplify both. The bar within the bar is accessorized by a canopy of 40 bike frames crafted by local custom frame builders. The frames add to the aesthetics of the bar's theme, but also serve, for many, as the only venue to showcase their innovative work. Light fixtures made from growlers, and constructed by students from the Pacific Northwest College of Art, hang down from even more bike frames attached to the ceiling. Two Plug-Out stationary bicycles sit at the front of the bar and actually generate electricity back into the building's grid when pedaled. Ninety-nine bottles of beer are featured on the wall—appropriately nestled in bike cages (how clever is that?). Aside from the crafty adornments that dress the space, much of the interior is sustainable and reclaimed. The table tops, bar tops, and wood paneling are all made from reclaimed materials, including the brick wall in the dining room.

Hopworks Urban Brewery installed low-flow toilets in their first location with an eye on the environment, and they stepped up their flush-savvy game with BikeBar's water closet. Stepping foot into this water closet is like entering a rainforest, sans the tropical birds, snakes and humidity. This bathroom boldly imparts the illusion of a rainforest with wallpapered walls of lush, green trees, allowing you to pee in a sleek, modern, and, most importantly, water-saving commode. The hand-washing basin is attached to the top of the toilet tank, which allows the water used to wash your hands to be smartly recycled into the tank for an eco-friendly flush. Now, while you may not hear any lulling waterfalls or rhythmic animal sounds, the peace and quiet of this eco-friendly water closet is priceless, especially if you are dining with or around small children.

Bishops Barbershop

If you belong to generation X, Y or Z and/or like listening to Run DMC while you toss back a cold one and allow a slick stylist to cut your locks, then this is the place for you. Owner Leo Rivera had a self-imposed goal to create a business of his own before he reached the age of 30. The outcome was this edgy "Poor man's social club"—more commonly referred to as Bishops Barbershop.

Incidentally Rivera himself is bald—so what does Bishops Barbershop mean to an entrepreneur who is bald? It's the culmination of a self-imposed aspiration and homage to his much-loved half Rottweiler, half St. Bernard who was affectionately called Bishop. Rivera's vision was to take this universal, albeit uneventful necessity of getting a haircut and turn it into an experience by submerging it within a bar-like setting.

Bishops Barbershop opened its doors to Portlanders in 2001. Since then, it has provided Portlanders with accessible style at half the cost of regular salons, while creating a cool buzz culture of its own—it is, indeed, Portland's original Rock 'N Roll Barbershop.

Here the decor is edgier, the music louder, and the conversation less conservative than at many other salons. Although each location has a slightly different vibe, you can expect to see a staff of tattooed stylists, an occasional DJ spinning tunes, and walls canvassed with magazine clippings. The walls may look like the product of a rebellious teenager who has decoupaged his room with pictures and phrases to agitate his parents, but most of these collaged walls do have a theme.

Every john within the Bishops Rock 'N Roll realm has some funky, eccentric thread or message that has sprouted within that personal space. Some bathrooms show a devotion to kitties, others promote fashion icons, and if you're lucky (in a weird sort-of-way) you might get the pleasure of peeing with the steely eyes of Jeff Goldblum and Christopher Walken peering at you.

Doug Fir

The Doug Fir is a modern, funky log cabin located on East Burnside, full of hipsters, strong drinks, and some fantastic music. Take a seat in the restaurant upstairs, saddle up at the bar, settle in on a couch by the fireplace, or sit outdoors on the patio where bamboo and fire pits intermingle to create an urban oasis. From the outside, The Doug Fir looks like a golden, glowing log cabin from the 1970s (think retro, not ramshackle).

Inside, the rustic lumberjack vibe continues with massive log walls, warm lighting, and unexpected modern touches, like a glass moose head mounted on the wall. Although log cabins traditionally aren't known for basements, the Doug Fir has a rockin' one! The Lounge hosts cutting edge concerts, and offers an intimate musical experience from every vantage point on the floor. Seven nights a week, a broad spectrum of musical genres can be heard here with ticket prices that befit a log cabin lifestyle.

The Doug Fir loo was the one that wooed me first—this bathroom was the spark that ignited my search for the best places to pee in Portland. I remember feeling both disorientated and wowed as I entered the bathroom. Jeffrey Kovel, of Skylab Architecture, designed this fabulous loo and has this to say about the design concept: "The Doug Fir bathrooms were designed with the psychedelic vision of dimly-lit dive bars with antique-mirrored walls, crossed with the more utilitarian function of the mirrored environments of the '70s." The bathroom's entire interior surface is enveloped with mirrors that have gold webbing throughout; the lights are the same golden yellow, and, as they skitter across the mirrored surfaces, they leave you feeling dizzyingly off balanced—in a someone-spiked-my-punch-and-I-liked-it kind of way.* And if you happen to walk in when the floor-to-ceiling stall doors are all closed, you can very easily be left thinking to yourself, "this is the craziest log cabin loo I've ever seen!"

* That dizzyingly off-balanced feeling can be multiplied to the 100th degree if you've already enjoyed a cocktail or two before walking into what looks like the internal realm of a disco ball.

B-Side Tavern

Tanya Podolske and Joel Denton are two friends who had a vision, thirty thousand dollars, and an invaluable army of skilled friends—these three elements came together to form the B-Side Tavern. The business' beginning was started with bare bones. When lights were needed above the bar area, they handed over a diminutive wad of cash to a friend, and artist, who specialized in welding. Wood boxes were crafted to frame old x-rays, resulting in a light fixture that captivates and illuminates.

Every nook and cranny of B-Side Tavern was crafted by the creative efforts of friends—and the bathrooms are no exception. Local artists, Tyler Corbett's skills add color and character to the walls in the ladies room, while Shawn Eschelman's art camouflages every inch of the walls in the men's restroom. As the murals become "enhanced" by bar patrons, they inch closer to becoming a fresh canvas for the next local artist to showcase their talent and express their vision.

B-Side is a place to chill with your drink in hand and elbows on the table. The bar also offers you a great opportunity to put your money where your mouth is by participating in an arm wrestling tournament for charity! The second year in business, Denton was diagnosed with Multiple Sclerosis. This diagnosis led to the creation of an arm wrestling table and the birth of "Ladies of Arm Wrestling" Tournaments, which raise money for people living with MS.

Some more amusing tidbits about the B-Side Tavern . . .
B-Side as in:
A) Burnside
B) Lesser known but cooler, like most B-Sides of vinyl records.*
C) If Portland was a record, the east side would be the B-Side, and downtown the radio hit.

* Some other B-Sides that boasted A-side billing: "I Will Survive" by Gloria Gaynor was the B-Side of "Substitute;" "Maggie May" by Rod Stewart was the B-Side of "Reason to Believe;" and "Single Ladies (Put A Ring On It)" by Beyonce was the B-Side of "If I Were A Boy."

Dig a Pony

Whether you dig a pony, dig bartenders that wear fedoras, or dig a really cool vibe, you'll dig the atmosphere at this Southeast Portland bar. Dig a Pony (DAP) is a place for trendsetters, dapper dudes, smart-looking lasses, and old souls. It was thoughtfully crafted by a young group of entrepreneurs—Jacob Carey, Aaron Hall, and Page Finlay.

Their goal was to create a warm and welcoming bar for the hip and sophisticated, minus the pretentiousness and high price tag that usually accompanies such an establishment. With the intention of being a "rad-pad" with sophistication, DAP's aesthetics can be described as a "turn-of-the-century, Northwest kind of affair." A beautiful horseshoe bar anchors the space. Vintage lighting illuminates the plethora of bottles that sit on the bar's wood hewn floating shelves, creating a fanciful focal point to the room.

In 1917 the building was home to Potter's Drug Company. The recent renovation uncovered beautiful old beams and the original tile floor that are now left exposed, adding character and warmth to this space. During the day this room fills with natural light from the two walls of windows. Punctuating the cozy library vibe are bound books tucked into shelves, beadboard backing the walls, a 110 year old piano, and custom stained glass work.

By nightfall, the room transforms from a quiet "library" to a multifarious room of 30-Somethings with contemporary cocktails in hand, mingling over the sounds of hip DJs spinning anything but top 40 music, seven nights a week. DAP may have a library feel, but it's anything but stuffy, and the bathrooms reflect its ability to balance the classic with the eccentric.

Enter the privy, where a soothing blue-gray colors the space, weathered-wood frames the antiqued mirrors, and a bold, custom painted Yak graces the wall—keeping a steady watch over the bathroom happenings. DAP embodies the lyrics of the Beatles song for which it was named: stop in and "you can celebrate anything you want. Yes, you can celebrate anything you want."

Header photo credit, Aaron Cohen.

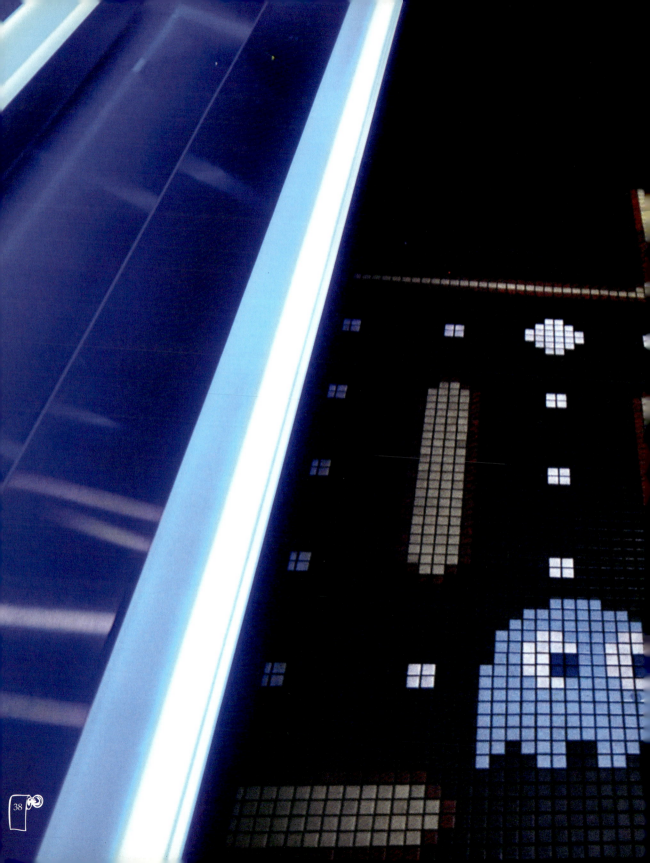

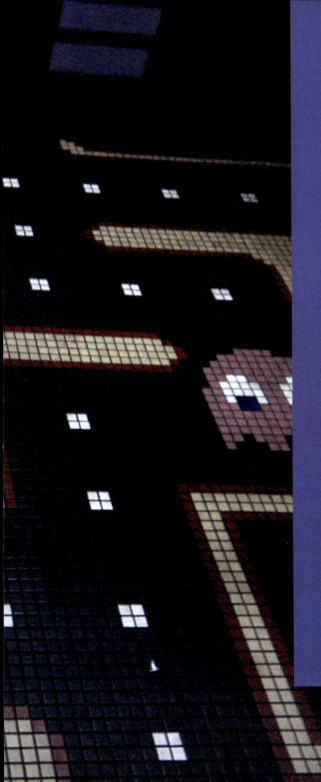

Ground Kontrol

Love video games and classic pinball games? Have you ever wondered what it would be like to navigate your way through one of those games . . . from the inside? Stepping through the front doors of Ground Kontrol is like being transported into the landscape of your favorite video game. Warm blue lights illuminate the space, while the iconic pings, wawawa melody, and spastic sound of flippers create a nostalgic playlist for your ears.

Ground Kontrol was founded in 1999 by two record store employees who loved video games. In 2003, five lifelong pinball and video game fanatics took over the arcade, moved it to a bigger space, and made some graphic changes to the interior. Thankfully, the bathrooms were not overlooked in this transformation.

Pac-Man and Ms. Pac-Man were the natural choice for "his and her" video-themed bathrooms. Over 96,000 one-inch tiles of various colors were sourced and meticulously arranged to create the authentic Pac-Man and Ms. Pac-Man grid that spruces up the bathroom floors.

LED lighting outlines the sinks and fades through an array of colors, from green to blue to fuchsia. From the auto-sensing faucets, fixtures, and lighting, to the precise imagery, it's easy to imagine you've materialized onto a game grid—and bathrooms turned out to be the bonus level.

The Observatory

An anchor of Southeast Stark Street, in the Montavilla neighborhood, The Observatory is the creation of two young couples who had stars in their eyes and restaurant experience in their back pockets. Looking beyond the bar's twinkling plethora of local and homemade spirits, you'll find salvaged church pews converted into banquet seating, and walls embellished with pictures of far-off galaxies and nebulae. Raining down from the ceiling, wires crisscross as if connecting the points of a constellation, each end illuminating a handcrafted light bulb that, when intertwined, shines like a cluster of distant yellow stars. Stargazing can spark your imagination and fuel your thirst for adventure. Quench that thirst with any one of The Observatory's hand-crafted, creative cocktails, such as the "Tom Kah,"

made with Thai bird chili-infused vodka, lemongrass cilantro, simple syrup, coconut cream, and fresh lime, or "The Remedy," made with house-made pineapple honey vinegar and champagne, served on the rocks.

Keep your sights high while letting the signs—restroom signs, that is—guide your way to the stellar water closets. At the end of the hall, you'll spy two restrooms that boast the same design, but with different color schemes. Flip the light switch, turn your gaze upwards, and behold a star cloud encircling the light fixture overhead. Colorful Christmas ornaments of varying sizes have been inventively arranged and secured around the light fixture, creating a "star cluster" that casts a soft halo of light over the restroom.

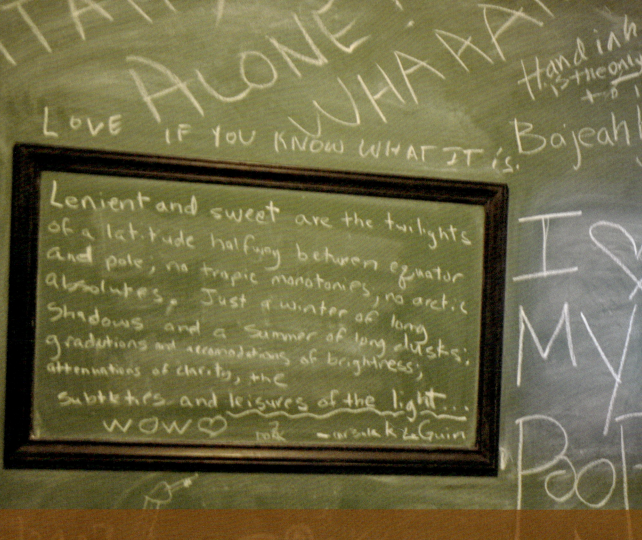

Over and Out

While the locals were sipping sublime cocktails at The Observatory, its owners expanded the borders of their galaxy and breathed life into a vacant space behind the restaurant, naming this adjacent bar "Over and Out." Slightly tricky to find, the easiest route would be to enter The Observatory, walk down the hall past the stellar bathrooms (see p. 40), through the door, and voila! You have now completed your journey, having travelled over to a new establishment, and out of The Observatory.

Over and Out is appropriately deemed the "sporty little sister" of The Observatory, with five pinball machines, two pool tables, eight beers on tap, and the same delectable bites and inventive cocktails as its ever-so-popular big sister. Siblings often emulate one another and Over and Out is no exception. With shared parents, the expectations for quality, service and atmosphere have been held to the same standards and the john in this spry little sister is no exception.

The chalkboard walls conjure up a cheeky type of humor and hipster inventiveness. Many restrooms in Portland have utilized chalkboard paint on their walls, but this loo went a step further by hanging frames, as if purposefully offering Portland's clandestine artists and bathroom authors a gallery for their art and water closet words of wisdom. The walls are washed down when they reach their capacity, so your masterpiece could live on for minutes, hours, or maybe even a few days!

Bastas Trattoria

Bastas Trattoria—a neighborhood favorite for over 20 years—resides in the distinct A-frame building that sits on the corner of Northwest Glisan Street and 21st Avenue. The owner and chef, Marco Frattaroli, regards his family and his Italian heritage as his greatest influence. Born in Rome, Frattaroli grew up in both Italy and the United States, spending time in kitchens that were filled with fresh ingredients, creative thinking and a contagious passion that come with authentic Italian cooking.

Lovingly hand-crafted meals are at the heart of this restaurant. An expert in charcuterie, Frattaroli was curing his own prosciuttos, salamis, and bresaola long before "house-made" became a buzz word. Not only are the ingredients local and organic at this charming Trattoria, the interior is also locally forged. The chairs were refurbished locally; the tables were designed and built a few blocks away; and salvaged barn wood was used to craft the tables, lending a rustic farmhouse chic to Bastas' interior.

Stroll through the wood-clad dining room down the hall to the second unisex restroom and behold the mysterious mermaid lady on the coral-colored fresco walls. She sprawls across three walls with such subtle grace that many patrons exit without ever noticing her. Perhaps she was painted in homage to the sea that supplies some of Frattaroli's favorite local razor clams and sardines, or maybe she's just a quirky artistic expression of the artist, who, incidentally, was once married to Frattaroli.

A handful of other inconspicuously painted, quirky images can be seen scattered up the tall peak of the A-frame wall, best seen from a seat at the bar—some may even make you blush. If you ask a bartender nicely, (s)he may even point them out to you. The authentic food and wine, local ingredients and décor are somehow even more delightful when served up in this peculiar A-frame building . . .

Departure

Stationed atop the historical Meier & Frank Building, anchored to the 15th floor of the swanky Nines Hotel, sits the bar and restaurant, Departure. Stepping off the elevator, you are immediately aware of the "barnacle" low ceiling and tunnel-like hallway that guides you to the bar and main dining room. An ocean liner motif fills this intimate space, with a wooden smokestack-shaped structure jutting up over the bar, which features sailcloth panels and teak decking. Glancing out and up from your helm-bar seating, you'll see a 65-foot long "windshield" skylight revealing the horizon—a view that cannot be beat. Venture beyond the ocean liner's cabin, and you'll find two decks to choose from—both offer sweeping panoramic views of the City of Roses.

Departure features contemporary Asian cuisine that utilizes traditional techniques and ingredients from the kitchens of the Far East, paired with the seasonal, local offerings of the

Pacific Northwest. The cocktails complement the culinary voyage through Asia with spice-infused libations made with Northwest spirits and local, handcrafted sake.

During this continental voyage, be sure to walk your sea legs to the "head" of this boat. The bathrooms are tidy and sleek. Low lighting swathes a row of geometrically shaped, metal sinks while two mirrored walls flank each end of the bathroom, creating the illusion of an endless corridor. For all of the reflective surfaces in this space, it's amazing that it always looks so shipshape.

In a place with adventurous cuisine, exotic cocktails and sleek, inventive design, Departure is Portland's one-of-a-kind, sky-high retreat for bites, mingling, and gazing off into the horizon.

Shigezo Izakaya

Shigezo is a Tokyo-based chain with its first U.S. venture on Portland's South Park Blocks. Not only does this restaurant offer your traditional Japanese cuisine—such as ramen, tempura and an extensive sushi bar selection—it also has a robata bar featuring grilled fish and vegetables.

Shigezo calls itself an "izakaya" (otherwise known as a pub) for good reason. Not only can you choose from a wide selection of sake, Shigezo has its own house cocktails such as the Godzilla, a Midori melon liqueur-based mix that puts you in a very convivial mood.*

While you're enjoying your Godzilla, it's not an uncommon sight to see groups of women whispering and giggling as they snake their way through the dining room headed towards the bathrooms. The ladies room at Shigezo has made quite a tingling impression on all those who have had the pleasure of using it. Why is that? Well, this toilet is not your everyday typical john. It is, however, a traditional Japanese "washlet."

This washlet can be thought of as the Rolls Royce of toilets (or a standby boyfriend when yours is out of town). With a heated seat, front wash, back wash, pressure and angle adjustments, it's surprising you ever see women at the tables in this restaurant!

* A very good point to iterate here is to avoid using "chin chin" when making a toast, since in Japanese this expression refers to the male genitals!

Zilla Sakè

Northeast Portland's Zilla Saké was borne out of proprietress Al'lowe's vision of an Ewok village teahouse tree house. Before opening this sushi house, Al'lowe was an artist and high school teacher with a background in anthropology and magic. She started her Northeast Portland sushi bar and sake house with the intention of creating an inspirational space that embodied the art and culture of its surrounding neighborhood.

Al'lowe's creative vision came to life on the walls of Zilla Saké. Its interior—everything from its hand-carved booth partitions to the lighting fixtures—is a collaborative endeavor by members of the Portland art community, lending the restaurant an ambiance that feels distinctive and organic.

Zilla Saké serves 80 premium sakes to explore by the glass, tokkuri or full bottle. The beautifully stunning and highly skilled sushi chef, Kate Sollitt, is lovingly referred to as the "Sushi Nazi," and she appropriately turns out strictly delicious sushi. This sushi bar and sake house has settled into being one of the most interest-

ing and economical spots in Portland to drink and develop your sake palette, while enjoying meticulously chosen and prepared sashimi, nigiri and maki sushi.

Even though Zilla Saké's all-black bathroom is located on Portland's Alberta Street and not on the Forest Moon of Endor, it twinkles with an iridescent incandescence, much like the glowing lights hovering in the Ewok village. The floor and wall are cloaked in iridescent black tiles and reflected in a fully mirrored wall, turning this bathroom into an exotic chamber.

Ewoks may not be your first thought when you enter this bathroom, but now that you know the background, don't let the fresh flowers and votive candles throw you—they may be used to distract you from noticing any of those cute fury little critters hiding in the corner.

The Deschutes Brewery and Public House

The Deschutes Brewery and Public House in Portland is the first facility to open outside the brewery's hometown of Bend, Oregon. The 10,000 square foot building in Portland's Pearl District was formerly an auto body shop built in 1919. The interior has been meticulously redesigned by the renowned local firm, Emmons Architects. Its original wood-beamed ceiling remains undamaged.

Seeded throughout the interior spaces are massive old-growth, reclaimed timber beams salvaged from a variety of local projects, including the old Meier & Frank warehouse, which have materialized as mantelpieces, tables and the main bar. The painted scrollwork on the exterior of the building that formerly advertised the makes of vehicles, now lists the brewery's diverse selection of beers.

The Deschutes Public House was crafted as a Northwest interpretation of a Scottish pub, but on a much larger scale. Intimate spaces were created using four timber-framed cubes that divide the space into smaller dining spaces. A wooden gate with scenes of Oregon wildlife, carved by renowned Sisters, Oregon chainsaw artist J. Chester Armstrong, encloses each smaller dining area.

The bathrooms at the Deschutes Pub were approached as an opportunity to make a statement. With the vast ceiling height and openness of the space, the plan was to source old large urinals, similar to those seen in P.J. Clark's, a famous old Irish Pub in Manhattan. After doing some research, the design team at Deschutes serendipitously tracked down a stunning double urinal in a salvage warehouse in Harlem.

It just so happens that P.J. Clark's had commissioned the porcelain piece because their old one was failing. The company that manufactured the replacement actually made two—the one in Deschutes is, incidentally, the second one. It has "P.J. Clark's" embossed on the upper corner of the right urinal: a source of pride for this unique establishment that manages to successfully pair rustic Oregon décor with an authentically Scottish heritage.*

* This past year while in Manhattan, I befriended a lovely couple and, after hearing about this project, they offered to show me their favorite bathroom in town. They walked me right over to P.J. Clark's! Incidentally, this occurred before I became aware of this Portland porcelain connection.

Metrovino

Whether you are a fanatical foodie or an oenophile looking for your next euphoric pour, hop off the streetcar along the North End blocks of The Pearl District and realize your passion at this elegant eatery. Metrovino is owned and operated by Todd, Jennifer, and Helena Steele. Pairing together an award-winning chef duo and trend-setting bartender, Metrovino sets the industry standards high.

The kitchen churns out refined, yet rustic and hearty cuisine, like grilled hanger steak with pancetta-wrapped fingerling potatoes. The wine enthusiast may get "tipsy" merely perusing Metrovino's staggering wine list, which contains over 90 sought-after and award-winning wines. An argon-charged Enomatic wine and Perlage sparkling system spans the wall behind the bar, allowing over 50 bottles of wine and bubbly to be kept "on-tap," tasting as fresh as a newly uncorked bottle.

The bone luge trend originated in Portland with Metrovino's very own bartender, Jacob Grier. It was a night of work-related gluttony during Portland's prestigious cocktail week when Grier, along with his festive and fearless dining companions, paired two delicious tastes together in a rather odd way—and it worked! What exactly is a bone luge, you ask? A drinker orders a crosscut, roasted marrow bone, eats the marrow, and then drinks top-shelf booze through the bone. This offbeat carnivorous means of consuming top-shelf liquor spread nationally from New York to Los Angeles. Grier recommends ordering a bone luge with a glass of "Contrabandista Valdespino," an amontillado sherry.

Before you start to look at your dining companion's femur as a potentially stellar liquor luging option, take a minute or two to admire the dining room where you're seated. Metrovino utilized repurposed materials, such as reclaimed wood and recycled carpets, to transform this urban space with fir beams and concrete pillars into something vintage yet modern. Rich colors and fabrics add panache, etched zinc table tops add flare, and the bathroom brings form and function together without neglecting style.

A collection of prisms plunge down the length of the horizontal light fixture, reflecting and multiplying their brilliance off the laser-cut grid that borders the vanity mirror. Modern sink bowls, a soothing color scheme, and tasteful art pieces round out the functional pizzazz of this ladies room. Metrovino is a restaurant and bar that effortlessly reflects the cutting-edge pathos of both the patrons it serves and the neighborhood it calls home.

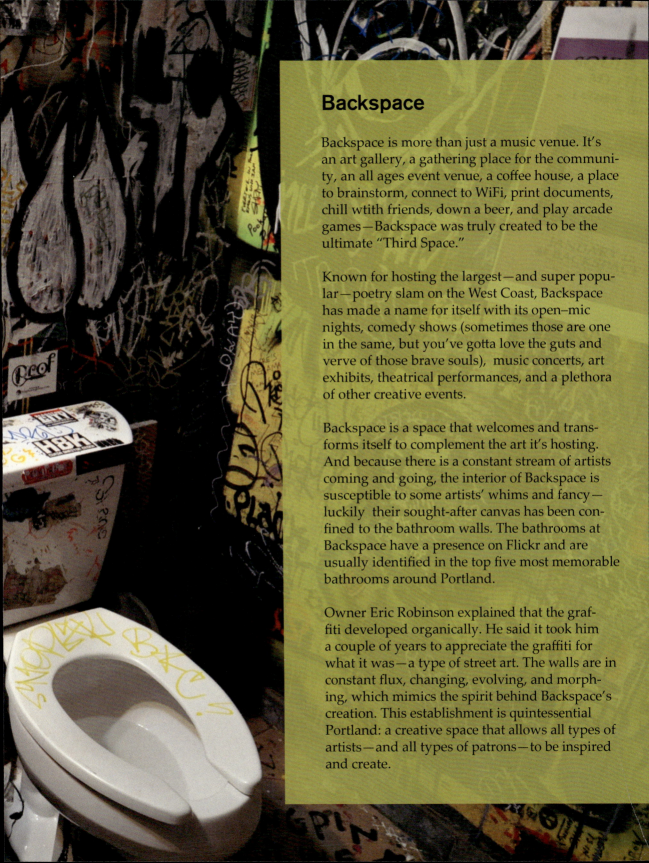

Backspace

Backspace is more than just a music venue. It's an art gallery, a gathering place for the community, an all ages event venue, a coffee house, a place to brainstorm, connect to WiFi, print documents, chill wtith friends, down a beer, and play arcade games—Backspace was truly created to be the ultimate "Third Space."

Known for hosting the largest—and super popular—poetry slam on the West Coast, Backspace has made a name for itself with its open–mic nights, comedy shows (sometimes those are one in the same, but you've gotta love the guts and verve of those brave souls), music concerts, art exhibits, theatrical performances, and a plethora of other creative events.

Backspace is a space that welcomes and transforms itself to complement the art it's hosting. And because there is a constant stream of artists coming and going, the interior of Backspace is susceptible to some artists' whims and fancy— luckily their sought-after canvas has been confined to the bathroom walls. The bathrooms at Backspace have a presence on Flickr and are usually identified in the top five most memorable bathrooms around Portland.

Owner Eric Robinson explained that the graffiti developed organically. He said it took him a couple of years to appreciate the graffiti for what it was—a type of street art. The walls are in constant flux, changing, evolving, and morphing, which mimics the spirit behind Backspace's creation. This establishment is quintessential Portland: a creative space that allows all types of artists—and all types of patrons—to be inspired and create.

Park Kitchen

Chef and Owner Scott Dolich picked a quaint location along the North end of the Park Blocks to open his restaurant in 2003. The name, Park Kitchen, was crafted to fit Scott's vision of a restaurant whose focus was inventive food prepared with integrity for the surrounding community whom he views as his extended family. Nowadays, with two successful Portland restaurants*, Scott spends his days sourcing the best ingredients in the northwest and training great cooks to meet his impeccable standards.

Like so many restaurants before them, Park Kitchen battled with paper towels clogging their toilets and wreaking havoc on the plumbing. People in Portland are known for their aptitude in creatively expressing themselves, and the staff at Park Kitchen is no exception. Fortunately, the office at Park Kitchen was adorned with nostalgic posters—this décor quickly inspired a clever solution to management's water-closet woes.

Jon Bon Jovi to the rescue! A poster featuring the musician switched residences from the office wall to the bathroom wall—with an added conversation bubble that reads, "Please don't flush paper towels in the toilet." Much to the delight of management, JBJ was a smash hit and not only stopped the clogged toilets, but created a little buzz of his own, as JBJ so often does.

That's not the only clever attribute that the bathrooms at Park Kitchen boast. Before the adjoining private dining space was acquired, the washrooms were in a shared hallway, and a nondescript door leading to the bathroom hall was visible to the dining room. In order to guide patrons to the restroom hallway, a local artist embellished the door leading to Park Kitchen's loos with a colorful (and demonstrative) "sign," featuring a bulldog lifting his leg to pee on a lamppost—a harmonious display considering the location of this restaurant and the dog-loving nature of Portlanders.

* Dolich also owns The Bent Brick, a contemporary tavern in Northwest Portland.

Morrison Hotel

If you're a Doors fan, you'll be smitten with the spot-on Doors album cover decal that adorns the Morrison Hotel Bar's front window. Inside, '60s rock memorabilia carry forward the nostalgic vibe. The bar boasts a stellar selection of over 100 different bottled beers and an array of pinball games. In addition, the space has flat-screen TVs that always draw a group of zealot sports fans who belly up to the bar to share in the triumphs or tragic losses of their teams.

There certainly is enough to keep you distracted from your date—which is clearly never your intention—but when you combine men with balls and beer, this seems to happen unintentionally. Your guilt over said date-neglect (in addition to past juvenile misbehaviors) takes over as you walk into the men's bathroom. Plastered on the back wall of this john is a request and a warning from Chris Joseph, the owner of MOHO, declaring in lipstick-red words to stop vandalizing the walls.

Joseph also reminds you that "the quicker you are out of here, the less time I have with your girlfriend"—spoken like a man who has reaped the benefits of bar ownership in more ways than one. So, order your favorite beer, play some pool, admire the rock memorabilia, but try not to imitate the bar's namesake* . . . and I'd think twice about introducing your date to the guy behind the bar.

* We can all agree that Jim Morrison was an icon whose music is rightfully worshiped, but let's keep the adoration and emulation there and avoid punching bathroom walls and/or overdosing. A bit of trivia: Morrison was caught repeatedly in venue and hotel bathrooms destroying décor . . . in addition, some say that the rocker died of a mysterious illness, while others allege it was a heroin overdose—either way, it was, indeed, in a bathroom.

Jake's Famous Crawfish

Considered one of the top seafood restaurants in the nation, Jake's Famous Crawfish has been a Portland landmark for well over one hundred years. In 1920, Jake Freiman reeled in this seafood restaurant on the corner of Southwest 12th and Stark Street, added the Cajun crustacean to the menu, and officially cooked up Jake's Famous Crawfish. Bill McCormick and Doug Schmick's 1970 purchase of Jake's—as it's fondly nicknamed in town—spawned a restaurant empire that now includes over eighty restaurants and catering operations.

Despite its name in neon letters on the sign out front, crawfish isn't the only thing that draws the crowds into Jake's; it's the wide array of fresh seasonal seafood that is flown in daily. Think salmon roasted on a cedar plank, baked scallops, Oregon Dungeness crab, oysters on the half shell, and pan-fried Petrale sole. Jake's also exudes the old-school grandeur of a Pacific fish house with wood paneling, white table clothes, and waiters that execute superb service coupled with a time-honored spirit of hospitality.

Jake's is a well-mannered establishment with the exception of the boisterous bar. It is in this cheerful bar that you will find an energetic buzz reverberating in the air. A mixture of locals and tourists belly up to the bar for hand-shaken cocktails made with fresh-squeezed juices and a much-loved happy hour menu that won't leave you or your wallet skinny. It is also here that you will encounter a visual historical account of "the ways from back in the days." As you take in the beauty of the rich, dark, original wood bar, steer your eyes to the base of the bar below the brass foot rail.

The green and white tiled mosaic inset at your feet isn't just a decorative element: it is actually a trough—a urinal trough. Back in the day, the bar was a place for men to toss one back and chat with other men, since women rarely frequented bars. During that era, it wasn't considered unhygienic or grossly inappropriate to unzip your fly and relieve yourself right where you stood at the bar! I will safely assume the majority of us are happy we have made such strides with our bathroom etiquette; and to answer your next question: yes, I have been told that, from time to time, a "funny guy" will indeed try to unzip, whip, and whiz.*

---

* I have coined my own name for these men: "Jake-asses." Feel free to use it as you see fit.

The Red Room

In H.G. Wells' gothic short story, "The Red Room," the protagonist reveals the room is not haunted except by fear itself. In *Fifty Shades of Grey's* red room, Anastasia is confronted by the fear, excitement and pain that Christian plans to unleash on her . . . Well, neither relate remotely to this Red Room.

The Red Room, set back off of Northeast 82nd Avenue, is a neighborhood dive bar that hosts punk, rock and metal bands. The facade of the building is drenched in an appropriately red hue. Enter this exuberant music box to a jukebox constantly looping through songs, Guitar Hero, pool tables, darts, and friendly bartenders. This intimate space is aglow in crimson colors, and the low ceiling hugs the sound in tight when the bands take to the stage.

Just beyond the musicians rocking it out on stage is a gallery of other well-known musical icons who have "mugged" for the camera—except these snapshots are actually mug shots.

The accent color of red complements the music typically played here: bold, shocking, angry, and loud. The punk vibe of the music correlates with the punk characters seen in this dive's

pissers. These characters colorfully and graphically radiate their peevish attitudes via their bad-boy mannerisms. Even if they don't offend you, you'll be sure to leave this john seeing red.

Old Town Pizza

Old Town Pizza is located in Portland's Chinatown; back in the 1800s, this area of town was known as the Old North End, a section of the city with a very questionable reputation. In 1880, the Merchant Hotel—the building in which Old Town Pizza currently resides—was built by two successful lumber barons and it catered to Portland's finest patrons.

In 1974, the Accuardi family opened Old Town Pizza in what was once the lobby of this historical hotel. The window where you place your pizza order is the original hotel reception desk, flanked by the original decorative cast-iron beam posts. Beneath your feet and below the floorboards of this space are the notorious Shanghai Tunnels. These tunnels connect Portland via underground pathways, and back in the day they were used to nab unsuspecting drunk sailors and transport them to ships waiting at the local dock. Often these vessels were destined for Shanghai*, where the kidnapped sailors would be forced to become slave laborers. Now these tunnels offer historical walking tours that detail their gritty and ghostly heritage.

Despite the Merchant Hotel's upper crust clientele, it was still known as a place that housed one of the oldest professions in the world: prostitution. As the legend goes, one of the "working girls," named Nina, was sold into the thriving white slave market of the time. Traveling missionaries, on a quest to clean up this area, convinced Nina to share information in exchange for freedom. Nina cooperated, but soon thereafter she was discovered dead after being thrown down the hotel's elevator shaft. Nina is reported to have never left the building. The remnants of the brick elevator shaft now serve as a "cozy" booth in the back of the restaurant. The booth has been characterized as sometimes feeling crowded, even when there is plenty of rump room.

The restaurant's transformation from the lobby of the Merchant Hotel created a bustling hangout for leaders in Portland's countercultural scene of the '70s. Actor Willem Dafoe could regularly be seen lounging on a couch in the mezzanine. Portland Trailblazer superstar, Bill Walton**, was known to ride his bike down from his house in the Northwest blocks to order his usual: a large vegetarian pizza and a pitcher of Henry's.

The bathrooms reflect the character and eras in which they were created. The original location is decoupaged from stacks of vintage magazines found in the tunnels, and they reflect the faces and adverts of those times. The tight and awkward configuration of these water closets are in stark contrast to the modern and spacious amenities in the newer location on Northeast Martin Luther King Blvd.

Back in the day, Old Town Pizza restaurants could be found in Salem, Eugene and San Francisco, but the original location in Portland is the sole survivor. Today the The Milne family keeps the Old Town Pizza legacy alive, nurturing a little piece of Portland's past and adding new facets, like a brewery, for the next generation.

---

* This is where the term "to get 'shanghaied'" originated.
** Walton used to reside off of Northwest 23rd Avenue and has ties to one other Portland porcelain locations, Spirit of 77 (see p. 100).

Hopworks Urban Brewery

Hopworks Urban Brewery (HUB) was Portland's first Eco-Brewpub. It was joined a few years later by its sprightly little brother, Hopworks BikeBar (see p. 28). Owner and brewmaster Christian Ettinger, takes great pride in and receives many accolades for his handcrafted organic beer, made from the freshest local hops and organic barley malt. The brewery itself is sustainably-built and operated: the original building—which, incidentally, used to be a tractor showroom—was professionally deconstructed and all usable materials were recovered, sorted and reused to create the sleek, modern structure that stands now.

A third of the framing material was reused in the reconstruction and all of the finish trim was constructed from recovered trimwork. The booths were crafted entirely from old ceiling joints, and the bar's foot rail is made from old boiler pipes.

The grounds host a rain barrel that captures water to irrigate their exclusively native landscaping. Even their delivery trucks use biodiesel fuel. The menu overflows with organic greens, dressing made from scratch (to cut down on packaging), organic Roma tomato sauce and, grass-fed organic beef. Hopworks is 100% renewably powered and "cradle to gate" carbon neutral. The 20-barrel brewery produces 11,500 barrels of brew a year, with ten different HUB organic beers on tap and two cask ales, 365 days a year.

So, grab a seat in a repurposed booth or prop your feet up on a boiler pipe, order a pint, devour a pizza, and don't leave without tasting a pretzel. In other words: do whatever needs to be done to merit a trip to these wonderfully whimsical washrooms. Ladies, if you don't enter this restroom with a "sunny" disposition, the message on this vibrant yellow wall just might change your frame of mind. The words, "You are beautiful" are gracefully painted backwards on the wall opposite the sinks, reflecting a lovely reminder in the mirror back at us women as we wash our hands.

Gentlemen, you need less reminding and apparently more sleep (or maybe just less beer consumption) because your john is outfitted with banana bike seats mounted above the urinals. Like so many of the other decorative details at HUB, these urinal-aids provide a comfortable, zany, and bike-centric place to relax while you take care of business.

The Jack London Bar*

Jack London is an American literary genius who is celebrated for brilliantly and compassionately portraying the never-ending struggles of man and nature. Millions are thrilled by his stories, and authors are inspired by his heartfelt prose. Many of London's real-life experiences as a writer, rancher, sailor, and gold prospector were richer than his fiction. This autobiographical cornucopia is what The Jack London Bar was modeled after.

What used to be an off-track betting parlor was reinvented into an eclectic space that now houses lectures, literary events, nerdy gatherings, art shows, and dance parties below the historic Rialto poolroom. A place that was once home to bright lights, long tables and old men watching races is now a space infused with creative energy that resonates with character and the desire to learn about a plethora of topics.

The ladies bathroom at the Jack London Bar went through its own imaginative transformation. The removal of the metal rectangular waste dispensers left gaping holes in the drywall; shadow boxes were cleverly installed to take their place. Rascal Johnson is the creative mastermind behind this project and she is a gal who has a not-so-secret love affair with flea markets and garage sale finds.

Her vision for this space was "Grandma who wears Hot Topic clothes" with a little nostalgia thrown in. Chunky pinstripes in warm burgundy, purple, cream, and black add pizzazz to the walls. Feather boas, sparkly tiaras, perm rods, and purple poodles oddly take up residence in these unique shadow boxes. A geometric shower curtain is used in place of stall doors and a black ceiling hovers overhead, successfully creating the "girly gaudy" vibe Johnson set out to create.

* As if a Grandma wearing Hot Topic clothes weren't intriguing enough, this establishment, like several others featured in this book, is purported to house a resident ghost. So check out their entertainment lineup and their oddly intriguing bathrooms, and perhaps you'll even get to experience your own ghostly encounter.
See pages p. 98 and p. 66 for more ghost stories.

Living Room Theaters

Who doesn't love to watch movies? Probably the same people who didn't buy this book because they are dull, dull people! How do you entice the everyday movie-goer to explore independent, foreign and classic films?

The Living Room Theaters answers that question by completely reinventing the movie theater experience with oversized comfy chairs, reasonably-priced candy and snacks, a full menu—and alcohol. Enjoy a pre-show meal in the lounge or saunter up to the European-style bar and enjoy a cocktail, beer, or glass of bubbly before the show. If you're having doubts about your film choice, order a drink to accompany you into the show. If you are already a fan, order a drink anyway and take a seat, relax and enjoy the beauty and comfort of this cinematic experience.

The Living Room Theaters preview a diverse array of film genres, including emerging local talent, film festival nominees, and even skype chats with directors. Oh my—I was so caught up in the foreign eccentricity of the place, I almost forgot about their clever bathrooms! The facilities are spacious and elegant with expansive granite sinks and a tasteful color palette.

The delightful deviation here comes while washing your hands or reapplying your lipstick.

The mirrors in the women's room are off-center to those hung in the adjacent men's room, with the recessed negative space between the two mirrors actually being two-way mirrors, creating a peek-a-boo effect between the men and women's bathroom vanities. So be mindful of what you pick, adjust or reapply, because it's not your own private Idaho. On the flip side, it can be seen as very avant-garde. It's almost as though The Living Room Theaters has set the scene for your own foreign film scenario, in which you explore the timeless theme of "boy sees girl in movie theater; girl notices boy in concession line; independently they go to the restroom, and to their surprise, their eyes connect briefly while washing their hands; back in the theater they look desperately for one another" . . . and, well, you know how that story goes . . .

The Secret Society

The Secret Society is not really a secret—and neither is their acclaimed Ladies Lounge. This gem is home to a cocktail lounge, recording studio, and ballroom, but the Ladies Lounge stands apart as perhaps the most beloved powder room in Portland. The owner, Matt Johnson, initially developed this space as a recording studio and music resource center. The building had housed fraternal organizations over the past 100 years and the halls echoed their rich history. After the opening of a small successful restaurant below this space—with diners milling about on the sidewalks waiting for a table and a bustling music venue adjacent to his space—Johnson knew he could showcase the rich history and charm of this 1907 building by offering a swanky lounge environment that could cater to diners and show-goers alike.

From day one of this design conception, Johnson knew that he wanted the establishment's menu, style, and function to reflect the history of the building, and the Ladies Lounge is indeed a reflection of its Victorian heritage. During the Masonic era, this room once functioned as the building's anteroom, where visitors—primarily the female companions of lodge members—waited to be accepted into the lodge. It's easy to imagine the room brimming with women chatting and exchanging gossip as they waited for their men to finish up lodge business.

Today the warm, soft pink walls, dark mahogany woodwork, oversized red couches, votive candles, and a vintage chandelier in the room harkens back to the jazz club era, when women would commonly ask their dates for money to tip the powder room attendant. On any given weekend you'll still find women gathering in this Ladies Lounge, primping in front of the gilded mirrors, or lounging on the cushy red couches while sipping a superbly crafted cocktail. When you visit The Secret Society Ladies Lounge, see if you can't feel a century's worth of past girlfriends right there in the room with you, ready to share a little juicy gossip or let a sister know when she needs to fix her hair.

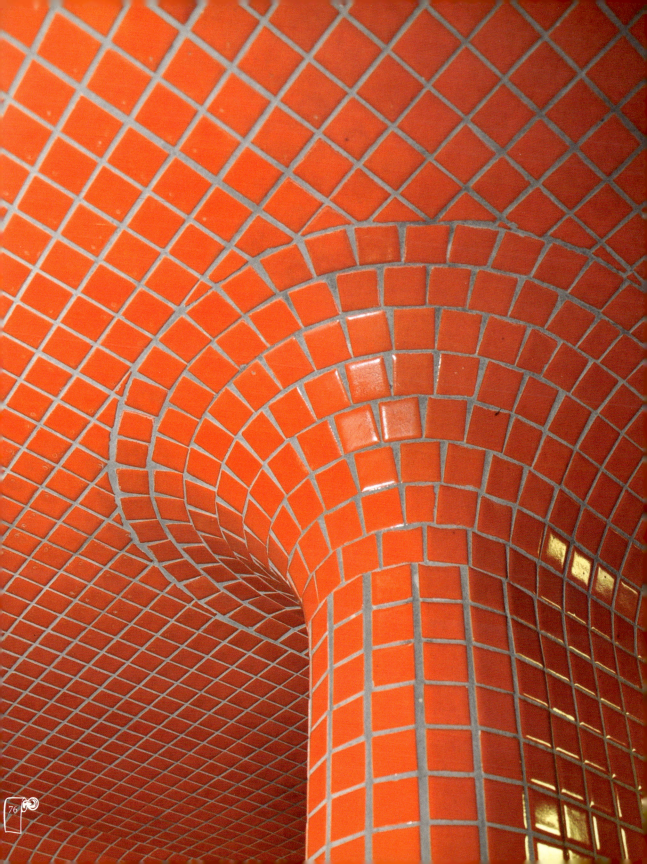

The Orange Public Restroom

I would be remiss not to highlight this bathroom —after all, this public bathroom has reviews on Yelp, pictures featured on flickr, and has its location and hours listed on two other websites. Located on Southwest 3rd Avenue and Clay Street, next to the cascading Keller Fountains*, this public restroom has been appropriately labeled the "Orange Public Restroom," and for good reason.

Tiny orange tiles dominate this restroom from ceiling to floor. Instead of the walls creating sharp right angles with the floor and ceiling, they unfurl into gracefully rounded curves that give this room an undulating feel. One reviewer likened it to the concept of being "devoured by a snake" as you wind your way past the smooth twists, turns, and curves of its internal pathways. To me, this bathroom holds less doom and gloom than some reviewers purport—I liken it to a brightly colored, slick waterslide with rippling curves that propel you down its track. To each his own interpretation of this orange-a-licious bathroom—just make sure you pop in for a peek so you can experience this acclaimed Portland potty for yourself.

* These fountains reflect the beauty of the art that is performed within the Keller Auditorium, and also provide a refreshing and fun place to frolic when Portland's temperatures heat up.

Crush

Remember The Ally McBeal show? It introduced us to digitally-created hallucinogenic dancing babies, the nervous nose whistle, nightly after-work drinks, the occasional sing-alongs with your colleagues, and—most memorably—the unisex bathroom. A late night Ally McBeal rerun, coupled with a limited space to build both a men's and women's handicap-accessible bathroom, helped foster the plan for the shared bathroom at Crush.

This Southeast Portland spot is a casual, hip neighborhood club that has a modern bar area known to serve up some of the tastiest exotic juice margaritas you'll ever encounter. Crush also offers up a plush lounge area, nestled just beyond the bar with gigantic colorful art on the wall, a stage for the occasional burlesque show, and a DJ booth for their almost nightly dance parties. Predominantly a gay bar, Crush is a place that is comfortable, classy, and sassy for people of all orientations.

Whether you're a man, a woman, a man dressed as a woman, or vice versa—it doesn't matter when it comes to the bathroom line at Crush. Three private bathroom stalls share one communal bathroom vanity area. The hallway leading into the bathroom lounge has a mounted chalkboard repurposed from a shuffleboard floor that was torn up during the space's remodel. Draw a doodle or leave a sexy message on the board to entertain future onlookers. The floor plan works brilliantly: dark walls and a vivid blue ceiling are illuminated with an art deco chandelier, while complementary blue tiles dress up the wall behind the sinks. Even on the busiest of nights, the bathroom line moves quickly and the women are not left to wait in a long line or have their girlfriends watch the men's room door while they sneak in for a quick tinkle. Since it is a shared bathroom, those who use it do seem to be neater and more respectful of how they go about doing their business, which is pretty potty perfect if you ask me.

Salt & Straw

Salt & Straw employs two key elements when it comes to making traditional handmade ice cream: rock salt and straw. Rock salt is used to freeze the ice cream and straw is used to keep the ice cream cold.

This "farm-to-cone" ice cream parlor mixes tradition with ingenuity. With flavors such as brown ale and bacon, pear and blue cheese, and foraged dandelion sorbet, "traditional" might not be the first word that comes to mind, but couple local ingredients in unexpected pairings with traditional techniques and you get one hell of a tasty concoction.

What started as a lemon sorbet cart morphed into two jam-packed ice cream parlors in Portland. Their ice cream is handmade in small batches, using the best local, organic and sustainable ingredients Oregon has to offer. Salt & Straw has indeed done for ice cream what microbreweries have done for beer.

Tradition, history, and artistry continue to mingle on the walls of the bathroom in this darling ice cream parlor. Owner Kim Malek unearthed a collection of postcards from a local resident, Miss Ada, dating back to the early 1900s. Miss Ada faithfully kept in touch with her friends both near and far via postcards that capture the time-honored tradition of written correspondence. The story that unfolds on the backs of these vintage cards captivated Kim and her crew. They loved Miss Ada's adventures so much that they turned the collection into wallpaper—now anyone who visits the loo at their Alberta Street location can share a few private moments getting to know Miss Ada, too.

Urban Farmer

The name Urban Farmer is illustrative of this establishment's ambiance, food and location. This restaurant is located on the lobby level of the posh Nines Hotel.* Stepping off the elevators on the eighth-floor reception level is like walking into a swanky modern art gallery. Bold, abstract, life-size statues are waiting in the wings, as if they're expecting their friends to ascend from the hotel's classically chic rooms. Beyond the registration desks, you'll find a magnificent, airy atrium, bathed in natural light that pours down from the glass ceiling. Intimately grouped clusters of seating are scattered throughout the space. Tall plumes of soft grasses and low stone walls delineate Urban Farmer from the shared lobby area space. The atmosphere is a balance of charm and rustic farmhouse elements, juxtaposed with the audacious structure of mid-20th century modernism. Despite its contemporary design, this modern Portland Steakhouse grounds itself in the philosophy of farm-to-table dining.

Pampered is definitely how one feels dining here and the powder room is a natural extension of this luxurious vibe. The high ceilings, tufted leather lounging ottoman, and an illuminated vanity flanked with a black lacey cut-out pattern gives this ladies lounge a glamorous feel. Cotton hand towels and aromatic counter products add to the age-old art of reapplying your lipstick in between courses.

Whether you are checking in to the Nines or checking out Urban Farmer, stepping beyond the registration desk is an experience that offers up a unique coupling of Portland's architectural history with contemporary Northwest luxury.

* The Nines Hotel rests atop the landmark Meier & Frank Building and pays tribute to the edifice's historical past. This fifteen-story, white-glazed terra cotta building was erected in 1909 as the flagship store and headquarters for Meier & Frank, which was once credited as the largest retailer west of the Mississippi. This iconic Portland monument housed the first escalator installation on the west coast and, incidentally, served as Clark Gable's place of employment prior to his illustrious acting career.

Scandals

One of Portland's most established gay bars, Scandals is located in the original "Pink Triangle" section of downtown Portland on Southwest Stark Street and Southwest 12th Street. When Scandals opened in the late '70s, the bar's name held a more literal interpretation; today, with floor to ceiling windows that let light and the curious onlooker in, Scandals is a very open and approachable gathering place. It is also one of the few places in Portland that boasts a winter patio. The patio's "living room" feel makes for a great place to drink and watch the world go by, get caught up in conversation, or simply hold your own court! Recently one Scandals owner, David Fones, donated his twenty-year-old deck so it could be repurposed into additional bench seating for this proudly open and out patio.

Not only is Scandals a great place to meet friends for karaoke, trivia or to dance—it's also a bar dedicated to its community. During Pride weekend, the sidewalk in front of Scandals is fenced off and transformed into an amazing block party that spans the entire weekend. Proceeds from the party go directly to the Cascade AIDS Project, which works to keep AIDS testing in local CAP bars free.

Scandals is a place where all walks of life are welcomed: laughter and memorable one-liners decorate every corner, and that communal essence carries over into their unisex bathroom. Painted a fiery lipstick red, the room features bright white modern sinks and gold-framed mirrors, evoking a sexy sophisticated elegance. With only a partition (aptly emblazoned with the word "Scandals") separating the commode from the sinks and the modern urinals, some patrons may find it quite "scandalous" to use the lavatory knowing others are just steps away.

Pink Rose

Venture below the fluorescent glow of Office Max, down a set of concrete steps and through a narrow dark door, and you'll emerge into a warmly lit, pretty pink, concrete cocoon. Pink Rose is a restaurant nestled away in an unsuspecting location in The Pearl District.

When Pink Rose opened, owner Adan Heller wanted a name that would communicate both a neighborly hospitality for their community and their reverence of Portland. Pink Rose embodied just that. In the botanical world, pink roses signify: happiness, elegance, sweetness, and gratitude. And for Portland—officially nicknamed "The Rose City"—roses rule. So Pink Rose blossomed into a perfectly Portland neighborhood bar with elegance and a darn good burger. The small scratch kitchen serves locally sourced food, cooked to order and made with love.

At Pink Rose, the décor is just as alluring as the burgers. Down the stairs and into this subterranean restaurant's unique, cavernous space, you'll find a ceiling composed of a series of concaved, concrete channels. Roses have been airbrushed randomly on the concrete ceiling to soften the urban undertones of this space. The intimate room is aglow with warm pink lighting, and velvet curtains soften the dining room buzz. A balanced blend of black-and-white art, coupled with pops of color, hang from the walls. An upstairs patio, complete with pink umbrellas, make for an ideal spot for lovely summer late nights sipping wine and sampling plates, or grooving to the tunes of a local band playing al fresco. On chillier nights, cozy up in the "cave" below and feel as if you are in a hidden speakeasy with classic cocktails and a very laid back vibe.

Head to this pocket of a powder room with its tucked-away door and you'll note the elegant continuation of the restaurant's rose theme. Aggregate black stone floors add texture and style to this small space. A beautiful hand basin floats atop an irregularly shaped countertop, and walls of mirrors serve to dazzle and duplicate the rose décor in this pretty little powder room.

Saucebox

The official definition of "saucebox" is a saucy, impudent person, especially a pert child. Walking into this Bruce Carey restaurant, you won't find many pert children; instead, what you'll find is a space that is bold, sexy and alluring. Sure, it gives off a bit of brazenness in its confidence as a hip, urban Portland spot, but certainly not in a childish way. The modern and clean-lined interior creates a beautiful canvas for colorful Pan-Asian dishes like the five-spiced cauliflower, green papaya salad, and sweet potato spring rolls. Saucebox, which opened in 1995, pioneered Portland's DJ-cafe movement, and it's still known for the variety of electronic house music, with DJ's spinning music five nights a week. House music on the turntables and house-infused specialty cocktails—such as "The kickboxer" or "The Diablo"—set the stage for a fabulous evening. The energetic vibe of the staff plays off well with the cool and clever customers who frequent this hot spot.

Mirrors that ebb and flow into one another create a basket-weave effect along the hallway that leads to the bathrooms. A Buddha sits philosophically at the end of the hallway, surrounded by votive candles, creating a sense of transcendence. An interruption in the mirrored hallway introduces this ambiguous male/female bathroom entrance: to the left, the ladies room, and to the right, the gents'. A beautifully massive flower arrangement sitting atop the faucet at the communal sink is guaranteed to draw your attention, diffusing its aromatic scent throughout this alcove. The real fun ensues at the crescent-shaped communal sink; if you happen to be in this dimly lit alcove with someone flirt-worthy (and hygienic), perhaps you'll slyly brush hands while washing—how saucy of you!

Olive or Twist

I prefer olives to complement my gin. Sam Fowler, the proprietor of Olive or Twist, is a fan of gin as well. The bar's name came out of a brainstorming session during which Fowler threw out a batch of martini-related terms; once olives were added as a garnish to the list of ideas, his search was over.

The pun on Dickens' famous novel is all the more appropriate considering the author himself was known to frequent gin bars. Nestled adjacent to Jamison Square, Olive or Twist has a clientele that ranges from young gin-novices and experienced martini-scholars to Pearlites and suburbanites. Whether you enjoy dinner or drinks and dessert, it's easy to feel comfortably indulgent in this classy yet casual space. Olive or Twist is as inviting and intoxicating as a gin martini.

The bathroom is a handsome extension of this distinctively elegant space. The space was small but Fowler was keenly aware that it deserved the same attention and finesse as the rest of the interior. A captivating black and white tile motif was beautifully crafted to add drama to this room. With two walls and a floor dressed up in this classic dynamic pattern, the opposite wall is mirrored to reflect, expand, and enhance this privy's pizzazz. The result: urban sophistication served up with your choice of an olive or twist.

Voodoo Doughnut

Since 2003, Voodoo Doughnut has been making some of the tastiest doughnuts in Portland and generating world-wide recognition. Voodoo now has two stores in Portland and one in Eugene. Each store has its own zany vibe that embodies the spirit of their doughnuts. Pink is the dominant color in these shops, with velvet paintings of Kenny Rogers, Isaac Hayes, and Conan O'Brian. Pinball machines, a photo booth, and a bubble hockey game add to the kitsch that decorates these doughnut dugouts.

So what exactly is all the fuss about? A sampling of some of the odd, mildly offensive, but always tasty creations: the famous "Bacon Maple Bar" (a raised doughnut smothered with maple syrup glaze, and topped with two crisp bacon strips); the "Memphis Mafia" (a banana fritter with chocolate frosting, peanut butter, peanuts, and chocolate chips); and the illustrious "Cock-N-Balls" (three raised yeast doughnuts artistically positioned to resemble "you know what," which are then triple filled with Bavarian cream, and finally topped with chocolate frosting).

Stepping away from the revolving glass showcase of doughnut creations and looking into the loo at Voodoo Doughnut Too, you will find "The Lady of the Loo," a papier-mâché woman wearing a mask, who is having her hair done by flying monkeys in preparation to meet the Voodoo King. And, of course, she has a doughnut where her heart should be.*

The vibrant mural that covers the surrounding walls is an elaborate masterpiece created by layers of duct-tape that have been precisely cut to reveal an energetic scene featuring tribal dancers and stunning Carnival characters. The bathroom at the original Voodoo has an equally fabulous '70s mod duct-tape theme adorning the walls (think "Mars-Man meets disco porn") Ms. Mona Superhero is the local artist behind these original duct-tape murals, both of which make it hard not to linger in these loos.

And if Voodoo, doughnuts, and duct tape weren't enough of a wow factor, let's throw in matrimony! You can get legally married at any of the Voodoo Doughnut locations. Already married? Don't fret! You can renew your vows under the holy doughnut.

* Terry Hallett-Lyman masterminded "The Lady of the Loo" and created the bust of this statue with the help of friend and Suicide Girl, Rachael Reckless.

The Rock Wood Fired Pizza & Spirits

The Rock Wood-Fired Pizza & Spirits is a family friendly restaurant bustling with energy in Wood Village, just outside of Portland. The building anchors the surrounding shopping center like a huge rock. Entering this space, you immediately encounter a sea of steel, exposed brick, and tall ceilings—evoking a slight similarity to that other "Rock," Alcatraz. But more on-point, you are surrounded by Rock 'N' Roll images that pay homage to many of the greats that filled our junior high record collection.

Opened in 1995 as a gritty local pizza joint in Tacoma, Washington, The Rock quickly gained favorable recognition with its wood-fired pizza pies, microbrews, and memorable ambience. Eighteen years later, dotting the map in three states and one foreign country (Canada), The Rock remains steady and strong.

Ladies, you will have to take these pictures for proof—or ask your man to stand watch at the door while you take a peek—because the men's room features an utterly unsettling design detail that can't be missed: grotesquely creepy urinals!* The Rock's first round of painted urinals, in its Auburn, Washington location, impressed the patrons, held their own up against urine, but they were no match for standing water.

A trip to a restroom in Spokane presented the answer for the owner, Brad Loucks: waterless urinals. Three new sets of custom-painted porcelain urinals were created to keep patrons on their toes—one for Wood Village and two sets for their newest Colorado locations. Portland is a city known for "keeping it weird," and so when the folks in "the rockies" poo-pooed the urinals as too wild, Portlanders welcomed these radical receptacles into their Wood Village location.

* The vivid facial expressions, such as the hilarious and utterly icky booger bubble detail, take these urinals from funky to fabulously unforgettable.

Escape from New York Pizza

"When the moon hits your eye like a big pizza pie, that's amore." Dean Martin crooned about falling in love in his famous song, and what ranks nearly as high as love on an Italian American's list? Food. Especially pizza.

Opened in 1983, Escape from New York Pizza was the first pizza-by-the-slice shop to open in Portland. The walls, counters, ledges and nooks are full of New York memorabilia and personal photos, lending it a no-frills New York pizza shop vibe. No charades here—just the confidence that comes with knowing who they are and what they do well.

The same talent and spunk that goes into the pies at Escape from New York Pizza is showcased on the walls of the bathrooms. Mike Scheer is a local artist whose work has graced the album covers of Built to Spill and local Portland band, The Prids. The bathroom walls overflow with Scheer's images, both big and small. Each image fits within its own compartmentalized space, unrelated to one another apart from their surrealistic nature. These whimsical fantasies of flight and imagination include flying saucers, bumble bees with top hats walking on stilts, animated red dots, graphically detailed obscurities and—my favorite—the massive eye that peeks so realistically out at you from behind the porcelain commode, miming the words: "Eye see you peeing."

The shop's attitude is as authentic to New York as its pizza. The owners and staff at Escape from New York Pizza thoughtfully put together a set of "Frequently Asked Questions" that not only educates patrons, but also supplies them with a dose of raw and uncompromising New York attitude:

Q: Can I customize my slice?
A: No. That would compromise the integrity of an already perfect slice. If you want Pepperoni and Pineapple that bad, you can order a whole pie.
Q: PLEASE! IT'S FOR MY KID!
A: Your decision to breed does not negate the need for pizza integrity. Besides, you are a better parent than that!
Q: Do you have Ranch?
A: No, Ranch is for salads.
Q: Do you have salads?
A: No.
Q: Why not?
A: If Phil wanted to eat salads, he would have opened a lettuce stand.

Slabtown

In the late '70s this Northwest Portland bar was a strip club called "The Dandelion." Legendary stories are still told about a stripper who was known for picking the straws up out of your drink without using her hands.* Then it became what was known as "Slabtown-the-junkie-bar," frequented by indie rockers and their hangers-on. After that, Slabtown became Cal-Sport, where westside Blazers fans could score bad cocaine. More recently, it was Slabtown-the-pinball-garage-rock-club. And now? Doug Rogers took over the space less than a year ago and, while it's undergone some changes, he claims that Slabtown's inner-dive-bar will always be in charge.

Rogers recognized no matter how much he cleaned, scrubbed or rebranded the place, Slabtown would always be its own entity with its own personality. This became even more evident when a smudge ceremony was performed inside the building. He explains: "as we walked from room to room and past every doorway, the smoke would not move but would only hang five feet from the floor as if it was held in place by the building itself. Below ground level, the walls and floors seemed to absorb the smoke. When we got to the old boiler, we could feel the bar's connection to the earth, its nexus. There was no purging the old there; we were held at stalemate. Back upstairs, we coaxed some of the ghosts into leaving, but even there, something was still fighting us. In the end, one of the ashtrays we were using to hold the sage exploded into shards. Slabtown was telling us that the ceremony was over."

The men's room is the place where you can hear the echo of "The Eternal Dive Bar" the clearest. Aside from the regular cleanings and icings of the piss trough, Rogers leaves her as untouched as possible: "There is no sense in taking down stickers from bands that probably don't even exist in this universe. Why paint over graffiti unless you're trying to create a fresh palette for more? When you step up to the trough, know that you are standing at an altar of sorts. You have become the Eternal Bar Fly."

---

* I'm trying to keep this a family friendly book, but you can use your imagination to figure out what part of the body a stripper would use, if not her hands. You can also read the full blog post "Slabtown" for all the details at www.thebestplacestopee.com.

Spirit of 77

Spirit of 77 is a Portland-centric bar for the ultimate sports enthusiast. The name commemorates the city's singular glory moment in sports history; in 1977 the Blazers won their only League Championship behind the efforts of their star center Bill Walton.* Inside, Spirit of 77 boasts an illuminated, vibrant orange "Spirit of 77" sign that sets the tone for this exuberant place. The theme continues outside the building with an oversized 36-foot sign that reads: "This is RIP CITY," the catch-phrase coined by the Blazer's beloved former play-by-play announcer, Bill Schonely.

This 3,000 square foot sports fan haven boasts four 55-inch flat panel televisions, plus a 9x16 foot projection screen dedicated to showing the biggest games of the day! The backwall of the 36-foot long bar is decorated with a repurposed basketball court originally used at Hillsboro High School. Twenty-eight bar stools plus another nine tables, each 10 feet long, fill the floor, but allow enough space for fidgety fans to sit, stand or pace as the fortunes of their favorite teams shift with the dwindling clocks.

Fan-friendly design elements place this sports bar in the upper echelon of game-day hangouts. Inside this A.E. Doyle-designed brick building is a Portland-centric bicycle parking area with a coffee and espresso dispensary next to it. A locally built "Buzzer-Beater" basketball shooting game is in place to accommodate the competitive patrons or nervous nellies in the crowd. Soccer fans take up house here as well. Pregame and postgame foosball matches ensue on the Rolls Royce of foosball tables, with a French made Renee Pierre Zince model that retails close to 2K!

When you need to take a break from rabble-rousing and beer guzzling, wander past the photobooth and you'll find another room where there's a competitive, albeit humorous, edge. The men's room takes a laughable approach to the concept "size does matter." Spanning across the distance above the wall of urinals is a mural depicting a wide array of sports balls and their respective size. So for those of you guys who've ever wondered how you "measure up"—well now you have a pretty good idea visually just where you rank!

* See how Bill Walton is connected to Old Town Pizza Co. (p. 66).

The Portland Loo

Portland and Portlanders are known for their creativity and ingenuity when it comes to design, environmental impact, and urban living. The mention of a public restroom tends to provoke repulsive looks on people's faces, but Portland has tackled that issue with an eye on aesthetics, safety, and environmental consciousness. The Portland Loo is a six-foot by ten-foot public restroom that is made from prison grade steel to ensure its cleanliness and longevity.

This ingenious public restroom was specifically designed to hold up well to the elements and its construction allows the entire building to be disinfected and sprayed down with ease. An anti-graffiti coating covers all interior and exterior surfaces, providing a force field against unsightly tags and other unsolicited expressions of art or anger. The loo operates off an electrical grid, powered entirely by solar-powered LED fixtures.

The only water faucet is located on the outside of the building, deterring lingering inside the loo. Louvered slats are placed at levels that permit outsiders to "see your trunk but not your junk;" this openness also allows the sounds from within to be audible to those close by, which promotes safety, albeit with the very real chance of occasional gastrointestinal noise pollution.

The Portland Loo has been installed in six neighborhoods, from areas populated with street kids to prime-real estate that is bustling with stay-at-home moms with strollers and tots wearing designer kicks. Its popularity and accolades have transcended the borders of Portland and has piqued the interest of city developers in San Diego, Vancouver, Houston, Baltimore and Seattle.

Its first official export was installed November 2012, in Victoria, British Columbia, and won "The Best Restroom in Canada" title sponsored by Cintas. The Portland Loo is patented and has succeeded in offering personal privacy, public access, and safety while fulfilling a basic human necessity. It's a toilet that is so popular, it has its own Facebook page, twitter account, and blog!

Bar Mingo

Holding its own on Northwest 21st Avenue, Bar Mingo emerged as an overflow space for its crowd-drawing big sister, Caffe Mingo. The space quickly stepped out from behind the shadows and took on a personality of its own, and Bar Mingo has now become known as a destination, and not just a pretty little layover.

Both establishments have garnered a reputation for dishes that please the palate with a consistency from the kitchen that is valued and appreciated. Traditional handmade pasta dishes earn the declarative, "delizioso!" followed by a sharp kiss to your fingertips. For owner Michael Cronan, this block of restaurants on Northwest 21st is a family affair, starting at the corner with Serratto, moving onto Caffe Mingo, and continuing onward to Bar Mingo, each one named after a much loved and revered family member. Cronan is the quintessential old-style restaurateur, who offers authentic, simple food and terroir-based wine pairings with a generosity that makes customers feel welcomed into the close-knit family of his restaurants' staff

Bar Mingo is swathed in warm tones of orange, cream and brown. Massive wooden barn doors, hung above the bar, add old world charm and a sexy masculinity to this space. The L-shaped interior creates two distinct dining areas; traditional tables and chairs occupy one while a generous "L" shaped banquet coupled with mini side tables creates another, more casually intimate dining space. Floor-to-ceiling gauzy

curtains and ambient lighting contribute to, as one reviewer aptly put it, "the buzzy boozy" ambiance of this space.

Whether it's the booze, your small bladder, or just an escape from a bad date that necessitates a trip to these powder rooms, once there, you'll encounter modern restrooms that deliver a punch of monochromatic color accented with bold white fixtures that pop off the vibrant hue of the walls. The modish tone captured my attention and I became instantly smitten with the juicy orange intensity in the first bathroom. My loo-love-affair intensified when I saw the azure color in the second bathroom. Orange is a color that appeals to the fun-loving nature of a person who likes a lively social environment. Blue or azure is a color that appeals to a patient, sensitive, persevering, steadiness and wisdom.

The vastly opposing—yet perfectly complementary colors—reflect the balance of these adjacent establishments. Whether you're an orange-natured diner looking for a casual culinary experience, or a true-blue patron seeking solace in traditional settings, your options are one doorway apart and the dishes will delight no matter which door you choose.

Oven and Shaker

An oven and a shaker are all you need for one hell of a tasty night! In case you're not familiar with the term, it roughly translates as a pizza topped with the perfect combination of delicious yumminess and a cocktail that quenches your thirst and seduces your palette—you'll find both here at Oven and Shaker. This modern urban saloon in the Pearl District pairs hearty Italian street food with ingredient-driven cocktails for a unique dining experience.

Oven and Shaker is the love child of four-time award-nominated James Beard chef Cathy Whims and verified cocktail veteran of the Northwest, Ryan Magarian. One has a passion for all things delicious and baked; the other has a passion for all things delicious and liquid. Throw in a restaurateur with a knack for success (local ChefStable founder Kurt Huffman) and you'll be happily sedated for hours. Once the food and drink coma wear off, test your skills at recreating your newest liquid love from the recipe that is printed on the paper placemats. No need to distract and swipe these placemats—Oven and Shaker gives them away!

Inside, reclaimed barn-wood lines the walls, while stainless steel glistens on the barstools and fixtures. The wood oven burns brightly in the corner and is said to be the Bentley of Italian wood ovens. The restaurant boasts a 45-foot-long wooden bar that is rumored to be the longest bar in Portland. The urban saloon vibe carries over to the restrooms with their warm and rustic reclaimed wood walls and farmhouse-style sinks. The bathrooms are sparse, but they complement the easy simplicity of the restaurant's urban saloon décor.

Stumptown Coffee Roasters

Cozied up next to the über-hip Ace Hotel on Southwest Stark Street is the handsome urban coffeehouse known as Stumptown Coffee Roasters. What started out in 1999 as a single roaster's revolutionary idea to brew the best tasting cup of coffee quickly took Portland by caffeine storm and has since spread across the country to New York, Seattle and Los Angeles. Carefully-chosen coffee beans are expertly roasted by coffee artisans producing a well-balanced and flavorful cup of Joe that satisfies even the finickiest of coffee aficionados.

At first sight the line of loyal Stumptown devotees can be intimidating, but it's worth the wait. These Baristas, with ink on their arms and vintage clothes on their backs, know their brews and can break down a coffee's attributes just like a sommelier can speak of the characteristics of a fine wine. Counter seating at the front window hosts a bevy of colorful people-watching opportunities. A doorway towards the back left opens up to the lobby of the Ace Hotel and super-soft-seating on their ultra suede couches, along with a vintage photobooth to capture those "before and after" caffeine glamor shots.

The single unisex lavatory is another innovative example of encountering uncommon, imaginative ideas within the confines of a commonplace necessity. Floor to ceiling mini, round subway set tiles parade across the walls all the way down to the gracefully curved corners of the room. A smart trim porcelain sink with an equally smart wall-mounted faucet catches your eye, while dark, smoky mirrors frame the room. If you should happen to take a seat on the porcelain throne, you will notice a slight reddish tint illuminating the dark mirrors.

Images that weren't present at first glance subtly come to the surface in a double-exposed manner, revealing moose, deer, squirrels, rabbits, evergreen trees, and even the Pacific Northwest's infamous Sasquatch. At first glimpse these happy wilderness critters appear to be frolicking within the mirror's surface, but some say they are doing more than frolicking. Want a definitive answer? Take a close-up peek for yourself.*

---

* Have an informed and/or imaginative explanation depicting just what those woodland creatures are up to . . . ? Post it on Portland's Funky & Fabulous Bathrooms Facebook page.

Index

Backspace

115 NW 5th Ave.
Portland, OR 97209
503-248-2900
Backspace.bz

 56-57

21st Avenue Bar and Grill

721 NW 21st Ave.
Portland, OR 97209
503-222-4121
21stbarandgrill.com

 24-25

Bar Mingo

807 NW 21st Ave.
Portland, OR 97209
503-226-4646
Barmingonw.com/caffemingo

 104-105

Atlas Tattoo

4543 N Albina Ave.
Portland, OR 97217
503-281-7499
Atlastattoo.com

 22-23

Bastas

410 NW 21st Ave.
Portland, OR 97209
503-274-1572
Bastastrattoria.com

 44-45

B-Side Tavern

632 E Burnside St.
Portland, OR 97214
503-233-3113

 34-35

Binks

2715 NE Alberta St.
Portland, OR 97211
503-493-4430
Binksbar.com

 26-27

Bishops Barber Shop
2132 NE Alberta St.
Portland, OR 97211
503-546-4171
Bishopsbs.com/locations/alberta

Deschutes Brewery and Public Ale House
210 NW 11th Ave.
Portland, OR 97209
503-296-4906
Deschutesbrewery.com

 30-31

 52-53

Casa del Matador
1967 W Burnside St.
Portland, OR 97209
503-222-5822
Thematadorbar.com

Dig a Pony
736 SE Grand Ave.
Portland, OR 97214
971-279-4409
Digaponyportland.com

 16-17

 36-37

Crush
1400 SE Morrison St.
503-235-8150
Crushbar.com

Doug Fir
830 E Burnside St.
Portland, OR 97214
503-231-9663
Dougfirlounge.com

 78-79

 32-33

Departure
525 SW Morrison St.
Portland, OR 97204
503-802-5370
Departureportland.com

Escape From New York Pizza
622 NW 23rd Ave.
Portland, OR 97210
503-227-5423
Efnypizza.net

 46-47

 96-97

The Gilt Club
306 NW Broadway
Portland, OR 97209
503-222-4458
Giltclub.com

 10-11

The Jack London Bar
529 SW 4th Ave.
Portland, OR 97204
503-227-5327

 70-71

Ground Kontrol
511 NW Couch St.
Portland, OR 97209
503-796-9364
Groundkontrol.com

 38-39

Jake's Famous Crawfish
401 SW 12th Ave.
Portland, OR 97209
503-226-1419
Jakesfamouscrawfish.com

 62-63

Hopworks BikeBar
3947 N Williams Ave.
Portland, OR 97227
503-287-6258
Hopworksbeer.com

 28-29

Living Room Theaters
341 SW 10th Ave.
Portland, OR 97205
971-222-2010
Livingroomtheaters.com

 72-73

Hopworks Urban Brewery
2944 SE Powell Blvd.
Portland, OR 97202
503-232-4677
Hopworksbeer.com

 68-69

Metrovino
1139 NW 11th Ave.
Portland, OR 97209
503-517-7778
Metrovinopdx.com

 54-55

Morrison Hotel
719 SE Morrison St
Portland, OR 97214
503-236-7080

 60-61

Olive or Twist
925 NW 11th Ave.
503-546-2900
Oliveortwistmartinibar.com

 90-91

Ned Ludd
3925 NE Martin Luther
King Junior Blvd.
Portland, OR 97227
503-288-6900
Nedluddpdx.com

 8-9

The Orange Public Restroom
SW 3rd Ave. & Clay St.
Portland, Or 97201

 76-77

The Observatory
8115 SE Stark St.
Portland, OR 97215
503-445-6284
Theobservatorypdx.com

 40-41

Oven and Shaker
1134 NW Everett St.
Portland, OR 97209
503-241-1600
Ovenandshaker.com

 106-107

Old Town Pizza
226 NW Davis St.
Portland, OR 97209
503-222-9999
Oldtownpizza.com

 66-67

Over and Out
8115 SE Stark St.
Portland, OR 97215
503-445-6284
Theobservatorypdx.com/
overandoutbar

 42-43

Park Kitchen
422 NW 8th Ave.
Portland, OR 97209
503-223-7275
Parkkitchen.com

 58-59

Rimsky Korsikoffee
707 SE 12th Ave.
Portland, OR 97214
503-232-2640

 14-15

Pink Rose
1300 Lovejoy
Portland, OR 97209
503-482-2165
Pinkrosepdx.com

 86-87

Roadside Attraction
1000 SE 12th Ave.
Portland, OR 97214
503-233-0743

 20-21

The Portland Loo
NW 11th & NW Johnson
Portland, OR 97209

 102-103

The Rock Wood Fired Pizza and Spirits
22401 NE Glisan St.
Wood Village, OR 97060
503-328-8498
Therockwfp.com

 94-95

The Red Room
2530 NE 82nd Ave.
Portland, OR 97220
503-256-3399
Redroomdvd.com

 64-65

Rontoms
600 E Burnside Ave.
Portland, OR 97214
503-236-4536
Rontoms.net

 12-13

Salt & Straw
2035 N Alberta St.
Portland, OR 97211
503-208-3867
Saltandstraw.com

 80-81

Shigezo
910 SW Salmon St.
Portland, OR 97205
503-688-5202
Shigezo-pdx.com

 48-49

Saucebox
214 SW Bdwy
Portland, OR 97205
503-241-3393
Saucebox.com

 88-89

The Side Street Tavern
828 SE 34th Ave.
Portland, OR 97214
503-236-7999
Sidestreetpdx.com

 18-19

Scandals
341 SW 10th Ave.
Portland, OR 97205
971-222-2010
scandalspdx.com

 84-85

Slabtown
719 SE Morrison St.
Portland, OR 97214
503-236-7080

 98-99

The Secret Society
116 NE Russell St.
Portland, OR 97202
503-493-3600
Secretsociety.net/lounge

 74-75

Spirit of 77
500 NE MLK Jr. Blvd.
Portland, OR 97232
503-232-9977
Spiritof77bar.com

 100-101

Stumptown Coffee Roasters

1026 SW Stark St.
Portland, OR 97235
503-224-9060
Stumptowncoffee.com

 108-109

Urban Farmer

525 SW Morrison St.
Portland, OR 97204
503-222-4900
Urbanfarmerrestaurant.com

 82-83

Voodoo Doughnut

22 SW 3rd Ave.
Portland, OR 97204
503-241-4704
Voodoodoughnut.com

 92-93

Zilla Sakè

1806 NE Alberta St.
Portland, OR 97211
503-288-8372
Zillasakehouse.com

 50-51

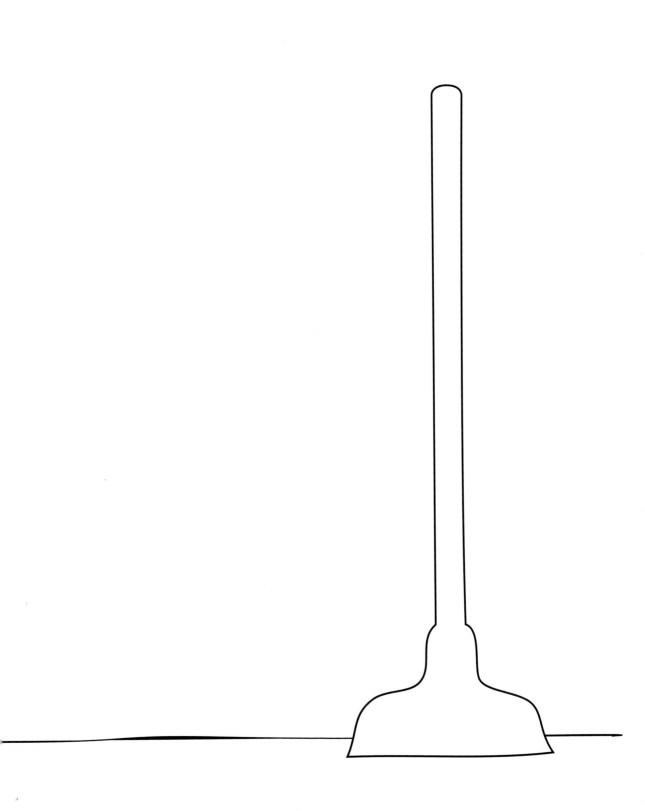

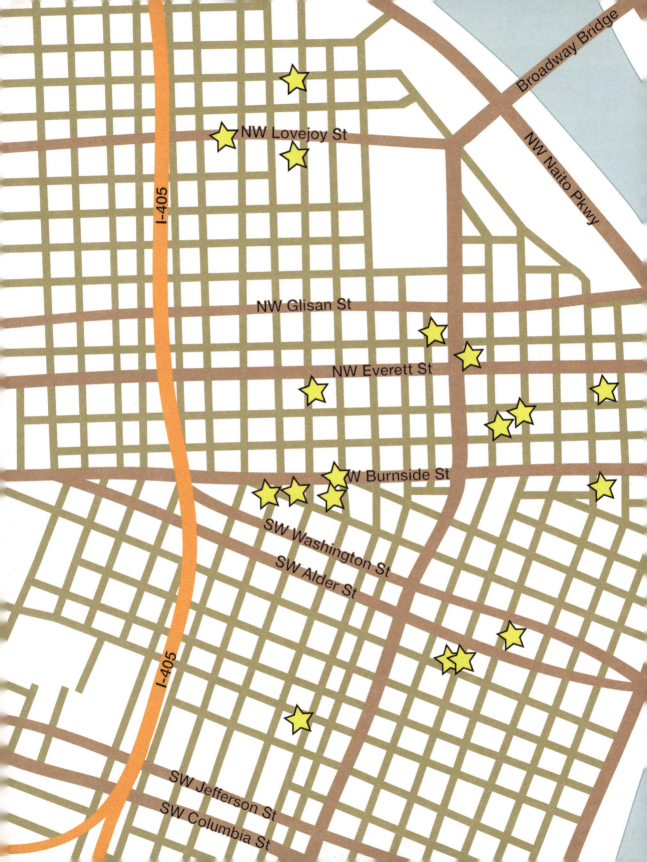